Sooners Forever

Sooners Forever

Coach Merv and the Stat Man

Dennis G. "Stats" Kelly

Deeds Publishing | Athens

Published by Deeds Publishing in Athens, GA
www.deedspublishing.com

Printed in The United States of America

Cover design by Mark Babcock.

ISBN 978-1-961505-03-2

Books are available in quantity for promotional or premium use. For information, email info@deedspublishing.com.

First Edition, 2023

10 9 8 7 6 5 4 3 2 1

For my wife, Elaine. Who loves and encourages me each day.

Contents

Introduction

The following are compilations about the lives of a legendary Sooner Coach and an accountant/stats guy who worked closely for nine (9) seasons on the radio for The University of Oklahoma football broadcasts. It also covers the interactions, stories, laughs, and the interesting things that happened over more than 100 Sooner games.

The original intentions were to keep track of all the fun times merely for my family, but I ultimately decided that others might enjoy it also. Coach Merv Johnson always said he could never author a book because "he did not want to move." I hope whoever reads this finds something of interest. My desire is you will find that no one is moving.

Coach Merv Johnson and Dennis "Stats" Kelly surveying Owen Field.

Mervin Lewis Johnson

He sits up in the booth so calm and so serene
knowing what's about to happen on the Owen Field scene
It's been years of steadfast working and amassing quite a fame
And we are so proud and happy, we stole him from Notre Dame
His voice has calmed so many, from players, coaches, and fans
Merv has the love of thousands firmly griped within his hands
He loves Oklahoma, the plays, and for sure the boys there
is a shout of glory saved for him and all the joys!

Psalm 112:6

For he will never be shaken.
The righteous will be remembered forever.

1. Glad I Took That Call

I received a call around lunch time in mid-August 2011. It was from my friend and former KWTV News 9 television station in Oklahoma City colleague, Toby Rowland aka T-Row. I was the Controller at the station and was so glad to see his name on my phone.

"Hey Dennis, this is Toby" (how my life was going to change).

Toby Rowland had been named the "Voice of the Oklahoma Sooners" earlier in 2011. He had left the television station as Weekend Sports Anchor/Reporter, and now worked for the University of Oklahoma and Sooner Sports Properties (Learfield). Toby and I had been friends for about ten (10) years or so. He asked me if I could help him with the stats for the OU football game, or that is what I thought.

(I had just earlier in that day told my wife that

I would not be going to anymore "live" OU games. I would just watch them all on TV. I said that I had seen National Championship games (in 1985, 2003, 2004, and 2008), the Rose, Cotton, Sugar, Fiesta, and Orange Bowls and would just stay home. Elaine said we should buy the PPV for the 1st game which was the Tulsa contest. I was thinking at the time as my cell phone rang about the dollars it would cost. I still remember where I was, you always remember the big ones.

My mind raced and I thought shoot yes, I could go to one more game if he needed me. I can do it for the Tulsa game. But Toby said, "No, I want you to do all the stats for me for every game." He said, "You would go to all the games and sit by me." At least I could go to all the games I wanted to attend. Toby did not know all about travel, and he said the pay was not much. But he would like to have me join him on the broadcast.

I said, "Well yes, I'm sure I would, but I need to check with my wife." He told me to do that and call him back as soon as possible. Within about 10 minutes, my wife said, "You said, yes, didn't you?" I called Toby back and was on the Sooner Broadcast team. I did not care what it paid; any pay was gravy and what a day! I had listened virtually all my life to Sooner football games on the radio. Bob Sr., Mike Treps, and John Brooks!! A staple in our house for decades, and I was going to be part of it. I really could not believe it.

Toby invited me down to OU on the 22nd of August 2011 for the annual "Meet the Sooners Sponsor" night. Introductions and a time to meet the coaches, Coach Merv Johnson, and the others. I had been to this annual event before as our company was a partner with OU and Sooner Sports Properties on the broadcasts. This time would be different. (This occurs each year usually at the Stadium Club on the East side, overlooking the greatest grass in America. The Sooner Sports Properties folks do this so the coaches can meet the clients, etc.)

My wife went to Zambia later that next week, so she could not attend. She went there to do mission work for a couple of weeks with my daughter, Kelsey, who served as a missionary there. I did have to leave our daughter, Denise, alone when I went to Norman, and I remember there was a big thunderstorm forecasted the night of the media event. It was hard getting home or even talking to her on the phone after the "Meet the Sooners night" event.

Toby had been a sports reporter/anchor at News 9, KWTV for 12 years. I had been a friend, helped him with a couple of minor financial questions, and talked sports with him for years. Luckily (for everyone, especially the Sooner Nation), he did not get the Thunder Sideline gig back in 2008. There was a contract dispute with his radio station, KREF, which he aired daily Monday to Friday at 6:00 to 9:00 am in Norman. The contract precluded him from getting the then coveted NBA job, a real disappointment at the time, but a blessing in disguise. Toby was crushed, but the best was coming.

It seems that when Toby got the play-by-play job, he had really no intentions to change the spotter and stats guy. The previous crew were to debut with Toby during the broadcast of the spring game in 2011 and had been with Bob Barry, Sr., the legend as he was known, for several seasons.

However, a fiasco apparently ensued. When the spring game started, Toby began calling the play by play on the Sooner Network, and the spotter began calling the game as well, into his ear. It was on the headsets that only Toby and the crew could hear, but was very distracting and caught Toby off-guard.

It appears that Bob Barry, Sr., had been taking direction from the spotter, due to his inability to see as well as he had in the past, and he used him to help with yard-lines, numbers, and whatever was needed. This went on for several plays until the first stoppage of play for a commercial. A Learfield executive who was there to check on things, watch Toby work, and visit with everyone, angrily chastised the spotter. He asked, "What was he doing??" He then informed him to cease and let Toby call the game. The tension was quite intense, apparently, and it made for a long day, I am sure. This needed to be fixed and at a minimum, drastically adjusted.

After the game, apparently days later, management of Learfield/Sooner Sports Properties who own the broadcast rights, told Toby he should formulate his own "staff" and get anyone he wanted to work with. And the result was Greg Blackwood was the spotter (Greg had told Toby earlier that year he would do it if he needed it) and me. And away we went. It was a little sad that the other guys were let go, however.

I got to meet the whole radio crew on that Monday night in August 2011 as the crew was introduced to the crowd of Radio sponsors after a big Head Country BBQ spread.

Michael Dean was the Producer-Engineer, Tom Shores on the sideline Parabolic Mic, Greg Blackwood of Channel 9 Photography fame was our spotter, and a new guy from Tulsa, Chris Plank, the new sideline reporter, were all there. Chris was the radio talk show/programming guy on Tulsa's 1430 the Buzz. I had been listening to Chris for years on the Buzz (he also had a Fox Radio National show) while in Tulsa. He is a real sports guy and knows about so many sports.

I ran into Eric Barnhart, the General Manager of Sooner Sports Properties at the venue, who I already knew. It was one of the few times I would see him not in Bermuda shorts. Toby's wife Jenni was there that night, and I had a nice visit with her as well. I knew Greg Blackwood, from News 9, but was going to get to collaborate with him in a different capacity. Initially we also had Chris Plank and Roy Williams (Superman) as part of our sideline group, though Roy did not attend the event.

Roy Williams did not talk much that one and only year (2011) he was in the broadcast group. He is a real celebrity and he mixed with the coaches and players, and it seemed to even "coach 'em up" at times. He had recently retired from the NFL and his love for the university and the Sooners was clear.

Toby was always asking Chris during the broadcast what Roy thinks during that first year, and Chris would say, "I'll have to find him." I am not sure he really wanted to be a working broadcaster. We all laugh about that now.

I do remember Roy standing in the broadcast booth at the Cotton Bowl—pounding on the glass looking at the Texas radio broadcast group next door and yelling "Texas Sucks." When you are Superman, you can do that. Those guys just looked a little sheepish to say the least. We won that 2011 game by 55-17 and he was right in that Texas Sucked.

Tom Shores was one of the only holdovers from the Bob Barry group (along with Michael Dean). Tom was a longtime caregiver for his wife Talesa, as she had MS and he had spent years virtually in hospitals, emergency rooms, rehab, and such. If anyone ever thinks they have it bad, they should remember Tom, and his sons Trent and Tait. They have endured for decades this terrible disease. They lost Talesa in June of 2018. She was a wonderful woman, and they had a great family. Tom is a great, energetic, and fun person, a God-fearing man and friend.

At the open house, I had the opportunity to meet Coach Stoops, and Lon Kruger, OU basketball coach, one of the nicest men. Other folks, such as Oklahoma Athletic Director Joe Castiglione, and numerous big wigs.

I then was introduced to the real hero of this deal, Coach Mervin Johnson. Coach Merv, as he was affectionately called, was about 75 years old at the time. He was and is, a coaching and OU legend. ***For this narrative, I will call him "Coach." When I say that, all the radio guys, OU players, OU staff members, coaches, and thousands of fans know what I mean.***

I remember the first things Coach said to me as he greeted me warmly. "He was just a walk on and now he is a motivational speaker" I was so awe struck that it took me a bit to realize he was talking about "Rudy" of movie and Notre Dame fame. Toby had been telling people that Merv had been the Offensive Coordinator at Notre Dame, had coached Joe Montana, and Rudy, and somehow Coach misunderstood who I was. Coach has trouble hearing, which is almost comical on some stuff. In retrospect, which was hilarious what he said about Rudy, but I was in such awe that I did not care. Coach was so nice and treated me with such kindness and respect. Heck, I was a nobody, and he is a legend. I was meeting a real live modern Barnabas just like out of Acts 11, an encourager and Godly man.

Toby used to comment on the air to Coach early in our time together that "he needed to write a book." Coach's comment always was, "I would have to move if I wrote one."

The actual idea to write this was born that day. To sit next to the man who was passed over when Barry Switzer was fired, only to stay with the Sooners for 513 games and become everyone's favorite assistant coach, beloved color broadcaster, and Sooner icon. It was the opportunity of a lifetime. I would chronicle the interesting things for myself and my family at the least. Maybe others, including Coach's family, might enjoy these musings.

Coach Merv was the guy who coined the phrase "Superman" in reference to Roy Williams. Merv and Bob Barry were conversing on the air after the famous play he had in the 2001 game in which Roy had elevated and hit Texas' Chris Simms. The play resulted in a ball being knocked loose for Teddy Lehman to intercept and score a touchdown. At 14-3, it was another Sooner victory and made game history. Merv referred to Roy as like "Superman." It stuck, and a legend was born that day in 2001. I have heard their discussion replayed often, and it still gives me goose bumps.

We all went over to the empty Press Box/Radio Booth after the meal and formal introductions. I was in such awe as I looked out over Owen field and realized how great an opportunity I had been given. Michael Dean said many times that a thunderstorm was coming. He is the resident weather expert of the group and often shows the radar on his phone. Greg Blackwood, Toby, and I were giddy in the radio booth and an approaching violent storm meant nothing to us. Tom Shores was having fun, but was an old pro. I took a ton of pictures on my phone.

I thought about my dad as I peered over the field and how happy he would have been. It had been sixty-five years since he had first seen this incredible sight. I had seats on the 45. Minimal pay (who cares) and an opportunity to sit between the "Voice" of the Sooners and "Coach." Two great Christian men added to a list of great influencers on my life.

Toby later that week came by the station with his daughter Chloe and gave me an example of the score/stat sheets that the former guy had used. I was looking at my OU resources and a Press Guide when they arrived. I said something to the effect that "Wahoo McDaniel is still in the OU record book." Toby laughed at that and told Chloe that he had chosen the right guy. We have laughed about that meeting a couple of times. I remember the puzzled look on Chloe's face. She laughed and said, "Wahoo?" Toby also told me then that there was a stat monitor that would be there in the booth too. Whew, I was relieved.

You cannot ever hide a person's true personality when you see them interact with their family. Toby is the best dad and is so gentle and a great Christian man and so respectful to his wife, Jenni, Chloe, Payton, and Trevor. What a nice person to hang your star on.

One of my first games in 2011 with Toby and Coach. I was giddy.
Coach was in the background probably looking at the O-line.

2. The Stat Man Gets Going Beside A Veteran

I asked Coach one of my first times to visit with him (before the first game I kept statistics) about a story I had heard for years. I asked him if he had said to Coach Switzer after the comeback win over Florida State at the 1981 Orange Bowl "there is one person who knew this (an 18-17 win) would happen." Switzer supposedly looked to the heavens and Coach Merv said, "No, Tom Osbourne." Coach laughed, "Yes, I probably said that. That is true." The legend is true.

The first game I did the "stats" was OU vs Tulsa at Owen Field with both teams running the spread and throwing on about every down. Things were hopping. I remember texting my friend Sam Moore and saying, "I am nervous as a cat." He texted back, "You'll do great." I appreciated that encouraging word. Toby said I did great, but I am not so sure.

(Plank's first game was against his alma mater Tulsa!) Landry Jones was throwing the ball all over the yard and he and the Tulsa QBs threw the ball 87 times. That used to be a season total!

Joe Castiglione, OU's incredible athletic director, also came into the booth like he will do for every game I have done stat work. He makes things seem secure and correct, despite his quiet manner. It is obvious why he is the best in America.

The stats were a challenge. I had an example stat sheet from 2010, and I copied it. The Sooners (and other teams) supplied a "stats monitor" with "live" stats on it as well which is usually about a play or two behind. The stats monitor was a monitor, an iPad, Microsoft Surface, or tablet. In the early years, I tried to keep all the stats. Rushing, passing, totals, penalties, etc. were traditional. I wanted to do it computer wise, but the old-fashioned way was the best. I could write faster than key in stuff. I began using mental math again that I had not done in a while. I had been using a computer or calculator to total up things for a long time.

It took about a year to decide that what we really needed is a glorified drive chart with passes, timing, number of plays in a row, etc. and especially passing stats and yards. We hoped these could augment Toby's call and hopefully deliver something a listener could not get anywhere else. I added a spread sheet to my info in my bag, and it has key stats like coldest kick off, postponements, over-time records, and attendance numbers. It also has weird stuff such as guys who have run, passed, and caught a TD — like Jake Sandefer who scored five ways; run, pass, catch, interception return, and punt return in 1957. These are what we hoped the radio audience would love.

In the first year, during a broadcast Toby said, "I don't think anyone thought that would ever happen." It was a ridiculous thing that happened such as a play. Frankly, I cannot remember, but I do remember saying "only OSU" and somehow that came out on the air.

This comment caused a turmoil and an apology letter. Figure that one out. Guess they do not listen to their own broadcasts.

Those who have never been involved with a live radio or broadcasting event cannot imagine what it is like to sit basically for about four plus hours with little break. It is a battle of the kidneys often (for me) and it is difficult to wait to go to the rest room. Often on the road the booth assigned is not readily accessible to the rest room, and the sensitivity of the timing to and from becomes important.

I do have to admit the seats for the games for our radio crew are mostly fabulous. Some are incredible, like Owen Field on the 45 and good like the Cotton Bowl around the South 20–25-yard line (depending on if home or away). Most of the away games can vary from about the 15–30-yard line to the back of the end zone, but are at a really good elevation. The price is right, also.

The booths can be very spacious like Texas Tech and Baylor to not enough room for two people, much less five, like the Cotton Bowl. Some windows open, like Owen Field, TCU, WVU, and the Cotton Bowl and some are sealed. Overall, however it is as Coach said, "pretty tremendous."

I try to recap what had happened each quarter for Toby via notes or on a small white board and keep notes about specific plays and actions. This often gives me less than a couple of minutes to make the bathroom run.

Often quarterly and halftime notes are tied to historic Sooner football statistics, sometimes broken, or tied within a game. We (Toby and I) always try to add to the broadcast and make sure that "OU Radio" is the only place you can truly follow the stats and Sooner lore. (I admit, the historic stuff, I remember because I was there or remember it vividly. One of the few benefits of old age.)

It was early in our time as a broadcast crew, I started bringing in leftover food that was uneaten in the suites usually near where we broadcast (home or away) after the games ended. It is food that no one is going to eat (minutes from the trash), and it can often be gourmet stuff. I always amazed our guys in the booth what the food can be. Often Toby will comment, "Wonder what Stats will find this week." It can be sandwiches, BBQ, finger foods, incredible cookies, and is appreciated after four plus hours of really no food or drink.

About the middle of the first year or so, Toby said during our pregame banter that we need nicknames. About that time or shortly thereafter, Greg Blackwood tripped down the press box stairs. He then became Greg "Trip" Blackwood. I do not think Greg ever tripped again.

We named Tom Shores "Jersey" aka Jersey Shores and then Toby and Chris started using the "Stats" motif and Teddy Lehman later on called Michael Dean "Dean." The nick names were all set.

Using my "Stats" nick name has been an incredible ride. I got that name in 2011 when I was over 55 years old. I am known by that by thousands of Sooner fans, and it always makes me smile. Finally got a name which really kind of sums up my years of delving and thinking about OU football, football stats, baseball numbers, and New York Yankee baseball lore as well.

The OU Sports information office has supplied e-mails over the years with exciting things I cannot remember or know (personal bests, obscure records). We use them to add to the broadcasts. I sometimes text my friend Mike Brooks (the official OU Historian) who has more OU information in his personal database than anyone I know. Mike is in the press box for the home games working with the OU sports information guys and he also goes to OU/Texas each year. I text him rarely at home games but often use his knowledge on the road since he is so amazing. Mike is working so much during the home games but not as much on the road games. He is home watching, and I use his incredible information and historical data.

I began my first year compiling some facts about the weekly upcoming opponents. This word document included information about the Sooners vs. the opponent, historical stuff and even things that I remember from live games or memory. I send one or two pages to the whole crew, Toby, Plank, Coach, via e-mail on Monday or Tuesday of game week. Toby told me one time that there is always at least one thing that the Sports Information Department office does not have. I take that as a real compliment. Coach has often complimented me about "some things in that deal I have not thought of in a while." I have done that every week except a couple since I started this gig.

Dennis Kelly at KSU with Coach Merv in the best seats in the house.

Pete Moris was the Sports Information guy for OU from 2011-2014, but went on to Virginia Tech. He was nice, but very secretive. He often would come into the booth and whisper that "So and so was out today" as the opening kickoff was happening. We always laughed at that one. Usually, Coach had told the news to the crew earlier.

Moris was replaced by Mike Houck, the basketball color guy who did a fantastic job with the basketball public relations stuff for many years. Mike is nice and a very no-nonsense director. Mike missed the basketball stuff, but this was a fantastic opportunity. I really like Mike and he manages so many people so well. It is a real machine with so many students and people working so hard on game days. I must admit, I miss him on the basketball broadcasts. Eric Hollier took his place and does an excellent job of supplying us in game tidbits, as we call it. He works coordinated with Mike Brooks to keep interesting things for the fans.

I have become acquainted with the man with the "pipes" that has been the PA man for well over 20 years at Owen Field. Jim Miller's "its football time in Oklahoma" line is familiar to all who go to the live games. He is an expert on older people and has the Savvy Senior syndicated newspaper column as his real job. He also does the basketball PA at Lloyd Noble for the men and women's basketball teams. Another little benefit of the job, I find.

The Sooners played Missouri for the last time as Missouri readied for their exit from the Big 12 after the 2011 season. We beat them 38-28 in Norman that fall, and I asked Coach about playing Mizzou (as a former Mizzou player and coach) and if it ever bothered him. He responded with a resounding, "No." This was the most definite answer I ever got from him.

Merv said, "Had the Mizzou job in around 1985 and left Columbia via plane with his wife with full intentions of accepting the job the next day. We went home, got the kids ready, told Switzer and waited. Someone, an alum from Kansas City, called someone else, and they never even called me back. Next thing was I heard they hired that other guy (never said his name)." By the way, the guy went 12-33-1.

It was obvious that he was ill-treated, and this was another instance of the Sooner's gain. Sooner Magic for all of us. Ironically, Coach was installed in the University of Missouri Sports Hall of Fame in 2021. The guy who got the job, Natta.

The radio guys in the pregame always do a "Countdown to Kick off" show, which had originally started decades ago when Bob Barry and Jack Ogle did the games on the radio. The tradition continued and would originate at the Fanfest outside the stadium before home games.

There was always a rush for the guys to get to the stadium after the pregame. That first year, I often went to the show with Greg Blackwood. When the show finished, we would hurry to Owen Field and the Press Box.

For one of the early games, we caught a ride with Roy Williams in a golf cart and streaked through the crowd as "Superman" waved to the fans. Coach Merv came to us later and asked us, "How did you get there so quick, oh, you guys got a ride with Roy didn't you, that explains it." Everyone laughed.

One of the first games was a game at Florida

State. Greg and I drove with our friend Terry Alexander from News 9. We drove her Cadillac and made the long 16-hour trek to Tallahassee.

While at FSU, we caught a bus ride with the trainers and team over to the pre-game walk around on the FSU turf. We got to walk around the field and see the players as they scouted the terrain. We took pictures and I got one on top of the FSU logo. Coach said, "I bet they loved you standing on the chief sign." I was such a novice; I did not know I was not supposed to stand on it. Coach just smiled.

I remember the press box distinctly at FSU. The consensus, from the comments I overheard, was that the Seminoles were going to win and how the fans would be rushing the field. These seemed to be support personnel, many fans, and not true press people. This seemed odd for a press box, with all the chatter about how to "save" the goal posts. We were decidedly outnumbered at the supposed pregame media meal.

However, the Sooners spoiled their little rushing the field party, beating them 23-13. Sooners have a real knack for spoiling fun like that.

It was a great trip, but we did get lost in the Florida panhandle on the way home, looking for 100 percent gas that Terry Alexander's car required. There were few gas stations then that had 100 percent gas. We were running on empty and found a station about 11pm that was closed. Greg thought we could get gas, hoping their pumps would still be functioning. We used a credit card, and luckily got about $1.00 worth and thus were saved until we found another station.

Ultimately, we had to use the gas with 10% ethanol due to the time of night. The car drove sluggishly with the lesser gas, but we found it ran great at about 85-95 mph. We drove home the 16 hours on adrenaline. (We had somehow been bumped from the team flight, but we were not going to miss an OU #1 vs FSU #5 game.)

Early in our radio arrangement in 2011, Merv was honored, and they went live from the "scoreboard video" to Merv in the booth. It was celebrating his 400th number of games with the Sooner program. He was so humbled and really did not want it to happen. People love this guy. I was in the shot, but really did not want to be there. I was as nervous as I can remember.

That was the time there were so many tributes coming in for his 400th game with OU. During the game, audio clips were run with Barry Switzer, Dr. Boren, and Bob Stoops, along with others congratulating Coach.

Later in the game, a touching tribute from his son Jeff was played. But at that time, Coach had taken off his headset and did not hear the nice, recorded segment. When Toby came back live, he said, "How did you like that coach?"

Merv quipped very matter of fact, "That was terrible," he was referring to the last play when the opposition had scored a touchdown. It was hilarious, and it was so difficult for Toby to not laugh. It was a classic.

Dennis Kelly with Toby Rowland and Chris Plank
at Florida State. Sooners spoiled their party.

The 2011 Texas game was my first one since 1990. My wife and I had been at the Cotton Bowl when the Sooners missed a field goal at the end of the game to lose 13-14. We had not gone back. I went in 1973, 1983, 1985, 1987 and 1990. We did not want to jinx them, so we nervously stayed home until 2011 when the Sooners won big, 55-17.

I went to my first OU Texas Game in 1973. It was Barry Switzer's first one and the Sooners beat the Horns soundly. It was one of the greatest thrills of my life and I sat around the 10-yard line with my friend Kim Arney, and we yelled until we were hoarse. The final score was 52-13.

Little did I know that I would someday be sitting between Toby Rowland and Merv Johnson in the small Cotton Bowl Press Box/Radio Booth looking out the dated storm window to one of the great spectacles in American sports.

The 2011 Sooners lost in a rain and storm delayed game to Texas Tech 38-41 which ended a 39-game home winning streak. Toby and Plank talked and talked and talked and talked through an almost non-stop two hour or so delay and when the game went back to play, Tech hammered us. We fell behind 31-7 early in the 3rd Quarter, and Landry Jones threw five touchdown passes (tied the record at that time), we just could not come back.

The real professionalism and talents of Toby and Chris were on display at that game. They kept the air waves hopping in an awkward and long delay. We only wished the team had done as well as they did in the broadcast. Coach told me he was really "proud of those guys."

There was this one guy who we watched during this game on the east side upper deck. He sat all covered up through the entire rain delay, storm, and lightning. I called him "Bombastic," and he was a trooper.

Coach said, "You were kind of hard on that fella" and then he grinned and chuckled at me. He thought I was a little nuts, and he was going to sit by me three months a year. He was right.

We were all so hang dog after the Tech game and Coach said, "There are things worse than losing a football game. It is not that bad, look at what these teams have done winning the 39. I can tell you in all the years I have been around this silly game, I have only seen two undefeated college teams." Coach was the sensible one, as we were all discouraged after a Sooner loss, especially this one. It was the first loss of our new "Radio Group." Coach is the all-time realist and optimist and was a solace for us as well as the sad fans listening on the drive home.

I visited with Coach for a long time in Manhattan, KS while waiting for the game with Kansas State to start. He said to me that KSU had players that OU could not get qualified academically, but they would have been a real asset for us. We had just lost a promising tight end that struggled mightily in the classroom who left the team that very week, and Coach was obviously upset he was no longer in school. "He could qualify up here, I am sure," Coach said. The standards for OU are so high, and he and I would not have it any other way.

The Sooners unveiled a short yardage package against K-State which featured Blake Bell. Coach just grinned when he saw it. He had seen them install it in practice, and it was unique in the modern college game, but was right out of OU's historic power run game annals.

The Sooners ran the second team quarterback Blake Bell five times on short yardage plays and scored a touchdown in a 58-17 romp. It became a crowd favorite and soon became known as the Belldozer. It was a formation designed by offensive coaches, Josh Heupel and Jay Norvell, to convert short yardage.

Bob Barry Sr. passed the Sunday after the K-State game in 2011. He had collapsed at home and was found unresponsive. He had broadcast the games for Sooners (and OSU) for years and had been personally chosen to be "the voice of the Sooners" in 1961 by Bud Wilkinson.

I am one of the lucky few to have spent hours working with two voices, Bob Sr., and Toby. I spent ten years working at KTVY/WKY-TV aka Channel 4, now KFOR-TV as Business Manager/Accountant and/or Controller. Bob Sr. was a big part of the station's success, and he was the Sports Director beginning in 1972 until he turned the reins over to Bob Jr. around 1997. Ironically, Bob Sr. became the Sports Director at WKY, when Mike Treps left the station to take the Sports Information/Media Director position at the University of Oklahoma. Mike also was the voice of the Sooners when Bob Sr. left for OSU, when the company Bob worked for lost the broadcast rights to the games.

While at Channel 4 (1986-96), I worked with Bob Sr's contract, which was a challenge. Lee Allan Smith, General Manager at Channel 4, had signed Bob up to be the Sports Director, with some interesting incentives, hopefully forever. KWTV, Channel 9 and the Griffin's (for whom I later worked) had made a serious attempt to hire Bob in the 1980's. Thus, the need for creativity.

I spent hours working with Bob Sr. and management smoothing all the contract particulars. Channel 4 was sold four times while I was employed there, and we had to navigate through the agreement with each of the ownerships.

Coach Merv became the color analyst in 1999 and he worked with Bob Sr. thru the 2010 season. Joe Castiglione had personally picked Coach to have the role and as Coach said to me, "I had no clue what I was doing, so I just talked about what I did know, football." Bob Sr. and Coach were great friends and colleagues, and obviously Coach was incredibly sad when Bob passed. The two guys were remarkably similar in their demeanors. Bob was happy and uplifting as is Coach Merv, and it always came through on the air that way, even in stressful situations for the Sooners and their fans.

Merv had spent years filling in for Coach Switzer on his daily radio gig in the 1980's. He was always available and did insightful radio interviews and recorded segments when Barry was unavailable. This certainly helped him move to the booth. He also, in the 2000's, did a weekly call-in interview on KREF Radio after Monday press luncheons.

He was so impressive and so good on these calls. He attributed it to the ease of hearing on the phones as opposed to the game broadcasts. I often had friends tell me they anxiously waited for the weekly analysis. It often was far better than the press conferences.

Coach said before the final 2011 Texas A&M game as a Big XII member, James Winchester may be the best overall athlete the Sooners had, "and he is a deep snapper, but could easily start at receiver." The Sooners were not as good as the 2010 year, but were bowl bound again.

In the second half of the A&M game, OU's Ryan Broyles made a cut on the near sideline and made his second catch of the game. He went down and Toby said on the air, "He looks like he is hurt." Coach said on the air, "Oh, he'll be back up." This was one time he was wrong. Ryan had torn his left knee and would never play as a Sooner again.

Ryan ended as the all-time Sooner pass receiver with an NCAA record 349 receptions, and 4,586 yards (with four games remaining). He leads as a Sooner receiver by over 100 receptions and 1000 yards for a career. Poor Ryan had basically ended his overall career as a player as he only caught 32 passes in the NFL.

OU (without Ryan Broyles) finally got beat by Baylor in 2011 on the "hit the guy on the helmet pass"- the signature Heisman play of Baylor's Robert Griffin III. It was quite a blow, until the Bears unraveled later in the decade. The Sooners had been 20-0 against the Bears, going back to 1901. The video of RG III throwing that pass was the highlight of the college season and was all over TV.

The Sooners had tied up the Baylor game at 38, electing to kick the extra point as a false start penalty negated the chance to use the Belldozer on the two points try and hopefully win 39-38. Coach whispered to us in the booth, "They should still go for two," but they did not. The Belldozer formation could not be stopped all night, but Baylor won anyway 45-38 on a late pass. In the first year with the crew, the Sooners relinquished their reign on the Big XII.

I secured my wife and daughter Kelsey tickets to the nighttime Baylor game. There is a misnomer that when you are on the radio broadcasts, as an "insider" to the program, that there are tickets all around. We got tickets to the Baylor game, but it was touch and go if I would ever get them. It is difficult to have family travel to Waco, or Lawrence, or any road game looking for tickets that may or may not be there. So, to put it mildly, I cannot easily get tickets, not even for my family. Sooner tickets for my whole life have been in real demand.

We did get to see Bob Stoops at the hotel in Waco. I had gone there to meet up with the crew and get my credentials for getting into the game. Bob was nice to my wife and greeted her with a "hello." He usually just nodded at me, or if I were getting on the elevator would say little. He is all business.

While waiting in Waco, I had an interesting discussion with Coach about Bob Stoops and his changes when he came to OU. He brought in "a strength guy," Coach said. Jerry Schmidt was the strength coach that Bob hired in 1998 to help turn the program around. Coach said he was "all business," and it was what the guys needed.

"Some of the coaches just about left when

Schmitty gave them their first work out," Coach quipped. The team was in such poor physical shape (to the standards they expected), that the assistants Stoops had hired were not optimistic that the team could turn around. They lacked discipline and the coaches were thinking about leaving before the new regime started. Bob Stoops had to do fast talking as the assistant coaches he had hired did not think the team could be saved.

Sooner fans everywhere are so glad he talked the coaches back into the fold and Schmitty, Mike Stoops, Brent Venables, Mark Mangino, Bobby Jack Wright, Cale Gundy, and others got it resurrected.

I did get to meet Grant Teaff, the legendary Baylor coach shortly after the BU game. I had read all his books and he was as gracious as I thought. He told me, "It will be okay, son," as I walked off in my OU shirt after the crushing defeat.

Coach Merv said, "He may have done one of the greatest coaching jobs ever, had harder academics."

He also worked with the NFL scouts, provided them with whatever they needed in terms of information or "film" as Coach called it. He would get excited when players were invited to the combine or when the seniors would play in the Senior Bowl.

Coach Merv and Kyler Murray on Pro Day, 2019

That first year, in 2011, he was excited about one of the Sooner offensive linemen. He talked to NFL teams about him, though he had not started much while at OU. Coach thought he had real potential. He was elated when he was drafted and went on to a career in the NFL. Coach was a true offensive lineman specialist. There were so many he helped land in the NFL, but he would never admit that.

Sooners were invited to the Insight.com Bowl in Tempe, AZ following the 2011 season. The Sooners walloped Iowa and Blake Bell had three TD runs. The midfield camera on a wire that was relatively new at the time came down during the game. I am not sure if it hit someone or not.

The only memorable thing was the press passes for the crew, held by a Learfield executive who had no plans to come to the game early, apparently. Chris, Tom, Greg, and I flew on the staff charter the day of the game. We arrived two hours before the game and Chris hurried to the press entrance at Sun Devil Stadium to begin the pregame show. However, no one had the passes for entry. Toby and Michael had arrived early from a Sooner basketball game via commercial flight and Coach had been with the team for several days. Toby and Michael did not have the passes and were already in the radio booth.

I got on the phone and called a cell number that Plank supplied for the person who apparently had the passes. I told the guy on the end of the line he needed to hurry up and get here, that we had an on air person (Chris Plank) that needed to be live and broadcasting. He was not concerned and said he would be here in a while. I said, "You don't understand. We need the passes so Chris can be on the **air now.**" He stammered around and said he would hurry. He finally apologetically arrived, and we got our passes, and all was good.

I was told later that I had yelled at one of the top guys and he may have had the last name of "Learfield." My response was he should know if he is in this business. Chris said it was "nice working with you." We all laugh about that now.

Every spring in Oklahoma used to bring us the Varsity-Alumni (V-A) Game, and now it is called the Spring Game and or Red and White game. A time when men begin thinking of stuff other than basketball and the bowl win. The game began in 1949 and covered 34 seasons as the Varsity Alumni, ending in 1982. It was an idea born by Bud Wilkinson to create a tradition and continuity for the supporters of the program. He and the coaches could see former players and use them to gauge the work needed by the varsity for the upcoming season.

The first spring game for me on the broadcasts was in 2012, and every year it is a problem (for me). There were few live game stats supplied by the Sports Information office and I had to keep virtually all the statistics. I am quick, but cannot keep up with every player, rushing, plays, players switching teams, and scoring drives. I am just not fast enough, and Toby and I normally zero in on a drive chart—trends. It is a stressful one-day deal. Each spring we need to know who performed, times someone tackled, quarterback stats, innovative scoring systems, and it can be difficult. There are often quarterback duels, receiver issues, et al. (The spring game can be competitive, and the Sooners are the only team in history to have two Heisman Trophy winners (Baker and Kyler) play in a spring game.) There was no talking in Toby's ears either.

The only redeeming feature for a statistician is the coaches want to hurry up and get the game over, having no one hurt, and go home. The only game ever played on Owen Field where no one cares who wins.

Each spring, Coach often would say he was unhappy about the way the "guys in the 90's" were lamenting. They had marginal success by OU standards, and they did not take part often in reunions and events centered around the spring game. Coach Merv was genuinely troubled and sad for them.

Varsity Alumni Game memories. I often remember Ronnie Fletcher each year rolling out to pass in his Bud Wilkinson Era white helmet, along with 1958 All-American Bob Harrison, who played over 20 times — against the will of his employer, the San Francisco 49ers. It was not unusual to see Steve Owens, Greg Pruitt, and countless stars of yesteryear defying the wishes of their professional clubs. It was a chance for the fans to see the stars and relive the memories and see them in the Crimson and Cream for at least one more time. I miss it and it has never been the same.

In 1966, Jim Mackenzie said he wanted to drop the game in favor of a controlled intra-squad game, but seeing so many players come back for Alumni week, he scrapped that idea and became a big supporter of the game. The overall record for the true Varsity-Alumni Games was Varsity 19-13-2. The Varsity won the first game, however, the alumni won eight of the first ten and until the early 60's when the AFL began surging and competing for players, the Alumni were 12-3. Beginning in 1964, the varsity won 15 in a row, with two ties. The 1981 game was the last win by the alumni and broke the losing streak that lasted from 1963-1980. A fellow named Dean Blevins quarterbacked the alums, as the alums prevailed 39-36.

When the USFL came into being in the early 1980's, there were virtually fewer players to take part as in the past, so Switzer and the sponsoring O club pronounced the game dead after the 1982 game. Switzer did really like the Alumni week and called it the most fun week of the year. He said, "That was only matched by the week after we beat Texas." Coach Merv loved seeing his players but said when "Mike Babb died in 1981 after a knee injury and surgery didn't help the game."

In the 1990's, the Sooner coaches and alumni tried to stage a game that was an incorporation of alumni into the varsity rosters in a somewhat controlled game-scrimmage. Touchdowns by Steve Owens, Greg Pruitt, and Joe Washington being the highlight of the 1993 "game". The 1994 Varsity-Alumni game was played at Norman High as Owen field's artificial turf was being removed and replaced with grass.

The broken ankle by long time Sooner fan and country star Toby Keith in the 1994 game at Norman High was one of the most unusual incidents in Sooner Varsity Alumni lore. Keith was playing defensive end despite the warnings of Coach Switzer. Coach Merv said they all warned Toby and Barry begged him not to play.

3. Some Changes

In 2012, we added Teddy Lehman and Dusty Dvoracek to the sideline reporting. They did an excellent job and made the sidelines fun and entertaining. Chris Plank blended in with them and it was really a sideline first, at least first ever at OU.

The first game of the year in 2012 was an opener at UTEP. We flew to El Paso and had a rare road game to start the Sooner season. I was jogging in 2012, and Coach mentioned he saw me out jogging in front of the team hotel in El Paso. Coach walks every day for about an hour and jogged or ran for years. He talked about his walking companion that "talks all the time we walk" each morning. Coach said he does not get to say anything, and the fellow just talks and talks. Coach said he tried to avoid him early in their routine, "thinking this may not work out" and go a different route, but "he stepped out of the bushes" and he has been walking with him now for years.

It was my first trip on the team plane. We met the plane out at Will Rogers Airport as the players and coaches arrived via busses from Norman and were escorted to the plane through the back door. We sat at the back of the plane, but I could care less. The plane was with Southwest Airlines and the flight attendants were so attentive. They were giving us food non-stop. It was the coolest thing ever. Greg Blackwood looked at me about 20 minutes into the flight and said, "You know we have not eaten in at least 10 minutes." The service was incredible and all First Class.

Mike Stoops returned to the Sooners in 2012 and retook the defensive coordinator position. Brent Venables left for Clemson and Mike had recently been head coach at Arizona. I rode on the bus right beside him on the way to the airport in El Paso. He seemed sort of melancholy and never said a word on the whole ride. He had been the man in Arizona and was now an assistant again.

I was not sure what Coach Merv thought of it, as he never really responded. He only said, "I think Mike came back to be with Brent." That never materialized.

Coach talked a long time about Venables while in El Paso. He said that he was really a good coach and was maybe in a spot to take head coaching positions but did not want the wrong one. Coach had waited and refused offers, and he hoped Brent did not fall into that trap and "be too old to take some of those really, really good jobs."

Coach Merv and Butkus Award winner, Teddy Lehman

"Brent may like the planning and hands-on, and not all the stuff that goes with it." Coach was exceptionally high on him and said several times he would make an excellent head coach. Merv was almost sure there had been multiple offers to Coach V., but he had not found one to his liking. "He has seen the bottom and the top at Oklahoma and even at K-State. That sure helps."

Coach sort of hung his head at the end of the Brent Venables discussion. It may have been a hope that he (Brent) would not let something get by and not get the big chance.

The offense had changed while Mike Stoops was away as Arizona's head coach, and now the Sooners would put up 50 passes a game sometimes. It was a different conference and even the Sooners were different than when he left in 2003.

In the 50-49 win at West Virginia in 2012, the three (Dusty, Plank, and Teddy) were dressed just like the coaches, as we all were in 2011 and 2012, but Coach Dana Holgorson from WVU complained to the refs. He said that our coaches were down on the goal line, out of the coaching box, meaning mostly Ted and Dusty. They were in no way coaches. Well kind of, sort of. Landry Jones threw for 500 yards vs WVU that night. Throwing yardage like that was never even a thought just years before.

In the WVU game in 2012, the first year in Morgantown as Big 12 members, former Sooner All American Joe Washington tripped a ref while on the sidelines and got a 15-yard penalty late in the game. Joe was so embarrassed. We will give him one, he brought OU a couple of big trophies. A nicer man was never born than Little Joe. Coach told us later Little Joe was devastated. He was on the sidelines to encourage the players, not hurt them.

Dusty, Plank, and Teddy were on the goal line

when Landry hit Kenny Stills with a pass (his 4th TD reception of the game and Landry's 6th TD pass, both Sooner records), to win the game 50-49 with 24 seconds left. The sideline guys virtually called the play, almost live (it happened so fast), and we celebrated what happened. Joe C jumped down on me and Toby as the pass was completed and we all had so much fun. (We did not know Joe was even in the booth.) WVU was ready to burn couches (their tradition), they had to do something else, but the fire department and National Guard folks were there. The elevation of the press box gave a view of the National Guard trucks and fire trucks coming over the horizon.

Dusty and Teddy went out to Lubbock in 2012 for the first time since being Sooner players. I remember walking on the street from the remote location and having crazy Tech fans yell from their cars at them "OU Sucks." Those fellows did not know who they were yelling at, these guys are not your normal size and had football credentials out the wazoo. They could have crushed those guys.

Michael Dean as engineer/producer did the wiring and microphone set ups, either at home or away. It is a mish mash of stuff and as coach Merv says, "Looks like a gang fight." It takes him hours to set up and he is so particular to ensure the broadcast is flawless. He will not let anyone touch the equipment. I try to act like I am going to touch the wiring and he goes crazy. I love doing it.

With all of Michael's broadcast wires, I have gotten to know Sooner Vision's Jacob Potter, Joel Manning, Dan Cavanaugh, and Craig Moore. They always seem to be around when all the stuff is being worked and tweaked. They don't know what I do, but I am always there, so they think its ok.

Michael is a historian and author. (Seems everyone calls him Michael Dean, never Mike.) He was a Marine and an Army Reserve veteran (go figure). He has been associated with radio and broadcasting for years and has worked in Public Relations for the Oklahoma History Center. When you see people listed as "Historian," well Michael really is one. PS, when you hear Michael say, "In 1968 or Beginning 1957, et al.," anything starting with a year, you will be in for a long story. It will be interesting, but you may have heard of it before. So, hold on, you have some time coming...

Michael Dean was with the radio broadcasts, both football and men's basketball, as the engineer/producer for well over 25 years. He worked for Bob Barry (the legend) and Toby as well. His number of games is over 1000 Sooner games for all sports. He has seen it all, travels anywhere at any time, collaborated with many coaches, and has sacrificed personal and professional time for the audiences of Sooner sports. Michael would do the lead to all the beer commercials. Toby was not comfortable doing those types of commercials since Diet Dr. Pepper was the strongest brew he had tackled. Since he was a preacher's kid, Toby would "just rather not do it," and tea totler Michael Dean complied. It gave Michael a chance to use his pipes which had been honed by all his radio experience since about 1964. (Too many Michael Dean's, but that is the way it sounds.) Michael always wanted to know our room numbers on the road. We always said we would not divulge that information and always enjoyed chiding him. It was a constant running joke.

In Lubbock, Michael, Toby, Coach, and Plank had to catch the team plane after the game, leaving Ted and Dusty to finish the post-game show. There was no number of breaks listed, and they just kept on broadcasting. Running break, over and over. Greg Blackwood and I stayed and helped them pack the stuff. I can still remember Dusty looking at me and saying, "Do we do another segment?" I shrugged and told him I guess so. Forty years in TV and radio, and I had never done that part of it, yet.

Dusty said, 'We can't really ever touch this stuff, and then Michael just ups and leaves." It was strange to say the least. It was an opportunity to razz Michael, which I can do quite well. It was so funny to be working with Michael, him in complete control and when they say the bus is leaving, he is gone. Those of us who drove packed up the gear. Now that is funny.

We soon had to dress opposite of the coaches in shirts in 2013. Then it evolved into whatever you want, home or road in about 2016. West Virginia's coach, Dana Holgorsen started that deal that lasted 2013-15. That 50-49 stuck in his craw and eventually wore off.

We went down to the field before the first game in 2013, and Greg put his mom's ashes down on Owen Field in the South End Zone. She had loved the Sooners and had passed that love to Greg. He had at times talked of listening with his mom to the Sooners with John Brooks and Bob Barry on the radio.

As we settled into the booth, I looked down at the South and there they were, a white streak of ash not very blended in. I at once said, "Look, Greg she's showing down there." It gave sad and happy feelings since it is where she would have wanted to be, I pray. What a son to do that for her. He is one of the kindest people. A no finer son.

I hope to have my ashes down on Owen Field someday, with Greg's Mom, Billy Vessels, and oth-

ers…And on every six or seven Saturdays in fall, you will think of me, maybe, maybe not. That is ok….

Greg Blackwood and his mom's ashes in the turf, 2012

Tom, Greg, and I were bumped off the plane for the 2013 trip to Notre Dame which was another game that you cannot miss. We drove up and spent the first night in Rolla, Mo. before our final trek to South Bend.

The woman at the hotel desk in Rolla was so happy to see us Sooners and she told us her husband was from Oklahoma and stationed at the Marine Base at nearby Ft. Leonard Wood. They were coming to OU later in the year for a game, so we got her a tour of the press box, and stadium, courtesy of our Michael Dean. We do appreciate the men and women who serve, and Michael gives a great tour.

The Notre Dame game was the first win of a Sooner team over the Irish since 1956 and makes our record at 2-8. Blake Bell had a great game and we won 35-21. We again rode home on adrenalin. (I bought the ball that Corey Nelson intercepted for a score, we went up 7-0 and never looked back. I proudly display it, despite the Irish Logo. I bought it through Steiner Collectables). I was so happy that I had been placed in this life with some of the finest group of men, not vile or rude, genuinely nice, to broadcast the great sport of college football to some of the greatest fans. God was good.

The toughest part of the Notre Dame game was hauling Dean Blevins' suitcase over the South Bend campus. Greg Blackwood told Dean we would take it back in my car, but unknown at the time, it had absolutely no handles on it. Try handling a heavy suitcase without a way to hold. That coupled with the visiting "media" parking was about as far from the press box as could be imagined. Ol Deano got to fly home, we drove, but luckily, the Sooners whipped the Irish. It is funny now, but not at the time.

Coach was so important at Notre Dame. There was a steady stream of people coming into the radio booth from Notre Dame "saying hello," honoring him. The Irish really revere the past accomplishments, and Coach Merv was a real link to those teams in the 1970's that hung a National Championship banner for them. However, it went from a wonderful day to a real low.

Later that week in 2013, Coach lost his wife, Cindy, to a brain aneurism. She had fallen ill as he returned from Notre Dame and our big OU win. Coach often spent the rest of Saturday nights in his office recliner to keep from "stirring up the dogs" and waking his wife. He would spend the night sitting in a recliner as opposed to his own bed after about a 20 plus hour day to avoid waking his wife.

On this occasion, however, she was unconscious and was in sad shape as he arrived home. He often did this when flying with the team, and he told me he "wishes he had gone on home."

Coach's wife was in intensive care for a short term, and he said to me when I went to see her, "She's going to have to alter her lifestyle." I saw Coach at University Hospital in those last days, as she lay in terrible shape. Coach was always an optimist and appreciated my willingness to pray with him and his son, Jeff, and daughter, Jan. He said that my encouragement really helped them. His encouragement and kind words made me realize I needed to make more visits to sick folks. I then added that to my own Deacon duties. Coach said just a visit of mere minutes can be so helpful and encouraging.

Cindy Johnson, Merv's wife of 53 years, passed away a few days later in early October 2013. The funeral was a real celebration and the outpouring of love for Cindy and what she and Merv meant to the Norman community, not just OU. Cindy met Merv when he was an Arkansas assistant and was a great coach's wife, mother, and grandmother.

Coach never missed a game and told me, "This is the best place for me. I just wish the rest of the family had football to get involved." He is a real warrior and kept on going. He did not miss a game in 2000 when his daughter Jill was tragically killed in a car wreck or when his beloved wife of over 50 years was lost. They do not make people like Coach anymore.

The Sooners have had very few changes to the basic uniforms over the years, and the 2013 Texas game was one of those rare instances. The two teams had gold "Red River Rivalry Patches" on their uniforms, gold piping of numbers, and the Sooners were upset that day in the Longhorns' Mack Brown's final Red River Game. Stoops is superstitious, and he never wanted to vary if the Sooners were winning (hotels and such). I do not think we will ever see those patches again.

I also went down to the locker room in 2013,

with Shores and Blackwood at around 6:00 am before the 11 am kick off. I got to try on the Golden Hat and walk around the Sooner locker room and walked down the famous ramp. After the loss, I decided to never do that again and to date have kept my pledge.

Coach has always said nice things about Mack Brown. He really liked his style of coaching and hated to see him leave OU after only one season. He was a little surprised, after he "retired," that he later went back to North Carolina, but thought he "really missed the players."

In 2013 we all went to Lawrence for the annual bout with Kansas. The once proud KU football program had fallen on tough times. Charlie Weis was then the coach, and he was collecting another paycheck. Coach Merv said, "He is a smart guy. He is being paid by three different schools (Notre Dame, Florida, and Kansas)." No truer statement was made.

The spotting job or finding who did what and who was in the game, scoring, rushing, can be tough. Schools try to vary their uniforms and many of them are exceptionally tough to see. The Sooners traditional uniforms and even the new "Rough Rider Bring the Wood" unis are the best and the most consistent and easy to call out for Toby. Greg Blackwood was the best I have ever seen as a spotter. He memorized all the numbers and would keep binoculars to his eyes for about four hours each game, quietly pointing to the numbers, accurately, on a spotter board for Toby to see.

The 2013 KU game may have been the most challenging spotting job in the history of college football. Kansas had white uniforms with white letters outlined with a "very fine" blue around the numbers. It may have looked cool on television or to wear around town but was virtually impossible to see at Press Box height.

I was walking through the Press Box returning to the Sooner (Visitor) booth shortly before kick-off and heard legendary KU radio voice Bob Davis yelling in a loud voice, "Why don't we announce to the world we don't give a hoot about football, look at those uniforms." It caught me by surprise, and I laughed aloud. It was true, and Bob did not care who knew. Bob did KU football and basketball on the radio for over 30 years, and this one was an all timer.

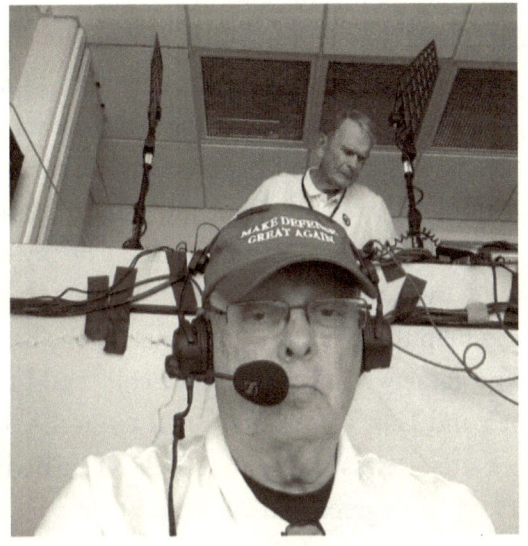

Coach preparing for the broadcast as Dennis
"Stats" Kelly peers onto the field

I had a heart attack on the Friday after Thanksgiving in 2013. I attended the OU basketball game with my daughter Kelsey and future son-in-law Brice. I was hurting so bad and thought I had the flu. OU was playing so well and were about to hit 100, but I felt so bad. I let Kelsey drive home and she knew I was sick when we left the game as they were about to hit the century mark.

My wife took me later that evening to the Oklahoma Heart Hospital, and I had open heart surgery on Sunday, December 1, 2013. I then missed my only game since the start of my stat career. The Bedlam upset that sent us to the Sugar Bowl later that week and ultimately a big win over 'Bama. I had great visits and calls from the radio crew while I was in the hospital, and I appreciated all the wonderful things Toby said about me. I have to say it was strange listening to the broadcast of my only true pre Covid absence to that date.

I did help them with certain stats for the broadcast. The game was played in bitter cold, and I texted Greg and Toby some notes I had about the coldest kick offs. It was the coldest kick off in Bedlam history at 16 degrees and the coldest ever for any Sooner game. (The previous record cold temperature was 19 degrees at Nebraska in 1993.) The wind chill of minus nine was the coldest ever too.

The Sugar Bowl trip was so cool, and we spent a few days in New Orleans. I also was able to go to the WWII museum, which was only blocks from the team hotel. Coach was standing outside the hotel in a drizzle, and I asked him if he wanted to go with me. He said, "No, I am waiting on one of my players so I can get him some tickets." He was giving a former player Sugar Bowl tickets. He was always there for his guys; he recruited them for life.

The radio group sat in the media area of the Super Dome and had dinner prior to the Sugar Bowl game with Alabama and OU. I asked Teddy Lehman as we were dining if the rumors that he ran a 4.3, 40- yard dash in wing tip shoes at the OU football camp was correct. He laughed and said no, that is not correct, but he did run a 4.38 for his first try as Sooner coach Mark Mangino was timing him. "The linebacker coach, Brent Venables, had said if I ran under 4.6 seconds, they would offer me a scholarship. I told them that if I ran slower than that I would take my cleats and leave."

Teddy said, "Mangino began yelling" and "whooping it up" when he ran his time. Teddy ended up running another 40 in a faster time. "Some of the coaches didn't believe it and were checking the times" remarked Teddy, but the scholarship offer was forthcoming. Teddy was one of the first commitments for Bob Stoops at Oklahoma. Teddy cancelled all the other visits he had scheduled and signed with OU. Brent Venables was his position coach, and the rest is history. One of the remarkable stories in all of Sooner lore.

I felt weak and sickly on the Sugar Bowl trip, but my surgeon and new good friend, Dr. John Randolph, was in New Orleans for the game and checked on me. Old number 87 (from his Sooner playing days) as I refer to him, is the best and I owe him so much. He saved my life. (By the way, he barely charged me for the surgery. I got the Sooner discount.)

Thank goodness I was there at the Sugar Bowl when Trevor Knight had his career day, and the Sooners took down the mighty Tide. Trevor became only the third Sooner QB to have two or more passes of 40 yards or more in bowl games and joined Ronny Fletcher and Sam Bradford.

I then got to see one of the all-time games in 2014 when Samaje Perine ran for 427 yards, the NCAA rushing record, against Kansas. It was something to see as he slogged through the rain. One thing about the Sooners...when they tee it up, you never know what will happen, and it can be legendary. He passed the Greg Pruitt Sooner record of 294 yards (at KSU) in 1971 that had stood for 44 seasons. I remembered that day too (via radio). Coach said he had seen, "Some things, but that was pretty special." Boy was he right.

Coach was reflective back in Ames in 2014, sitting in the press box waiting for the game. He said to me, "We have a few adjustments we could do offensively." We were struggling and finished 8-5. "I think I could help them (Josh Heupel), but I don't think they will ask." They never did ask, and the rest is history. Coach always goes to the coaches' box on the road trips and sits in there alone. When I find him, he will give me real nuggets of knowledge and insight. Interestingly, people pay big money for leadership ideas he gives me freely.

Coach Merv and Toby Rowland at Meet the Sooners in 2015

Dusty Dvoracek left us for The Sports Animal radio and ESPN after 2014. There was turmoil that I was not privy to. Dusty had parlayed this gig later into an ESPN TV deal. He was smart and missed when he left, but it gave Ted a chance to really shine. Dusty was a confident orator and his leaving worked to make Ted better. He was missed and is a great guy and is on to more fame and fortune. He is still a friend, and we get to see him from time to time.

In 2015, Learfield and OU talked Chris Plank

into leaving the Tulsa area and moving to Norman. He had been in Tulsa for many years and had been doing radio in that market since graduating from the University of Tulsa. The Sooners wanted him to come to Norman, and along with his sideline duties help start a radio and internet streaming presence for the Sooner Women's softball juggernaut. Chris grabbed this opportunity to be one of the first universities to embrace Women's softball in this way. He is now the voice of Oklahoma Women's Softball. He still does his national Fox Sports Radio show with Arnie Spanier early Sunday mornings and has numerous podcasts, Fox Sports radio shows, KREF Radio show, and Sirus XM gigs. He is a radio workhorse, and as Coach said, "Chis is all over the radio."

The Sooners played at The University of Tennessee in Knoxville in 2015. I remember Coach talking about the stadium and the punter. "We got to watch the punter for Tennessee. That guy impressed me." He was right, it was a Colquitt, another in an extensive line of Colquitt's for the Volunteers. It was Coach's first time seeing Neyland stadium.

Neyland Stadium had a large sign saying, "National Champions 1967". I pointed it out to Teddy Lehman and said, "We beat them in 1967 (Orange Bowl, 26-24). How did that happen?"

Teddy said, "Must be some flower club." It was the Litkenhous National Championship, hardly an AP or consensus, and was close to a flower club. Their championship was awarded before the bowl games. (Oklahoma does not accept any but the AP as a true National Championship.)

Early in the Tennessee game, Baker Mayfield was struggling. The fans were getting restless, and there was, I am sure, a sense of urgency as Trevor Knight was still available on the sideline. But then, Baker made his legendary comeback to win in double OT as we were down 17-3 going into the 4th quarter. The legend of Baker Mayfield and his knack for drama was born. Sterling Shepherd made a spectacular catch and run. One of the greatest comebacks in OU history ensued. OU President David Boren came into the broadcast booth after the big Tennessee win and went on the air to address "Sooners everywhere." Coach said to me, "We don't get that very often." What a thrilling and spectacular night.

Coach was there when OU came back from the 20-3 deficit at OSU in 1983. Coach told me if our kicker, Tim Lashar, had not missed the kick-off that hit that guy in the head on the onside kick, we would not have won that one, this one feels about the same." OU won 21-20 in that OSU game.

He also said, "I've been with those Shepherd

boys a lot." Coach had coached Derrick in the 1983 game, and now his son helped us beat a mighty SEC team. "Darrell (Sterling's uncle) was pretty special too," Coach quipped.

We added Rufus Alexander, former All-American linebacker, and Big 12 Defensive Player of the Year, as an analyst in our Post Game and Pre-Game broadcast in 2015. A more fun guy cannot be found than Rufus. He is famous for just showing up at our out-of-town venues and he is forever having credential problems. Somehow Eric Barnhart forgets him, and we sneak him in venues as someone else. No one does not like Rufus. Rufus did miss the flight home after the 2017 Sugar Bowl in New Orleans and had to take the 14-hour band bus ride back to Norman. We all laughed at that one. Rufus said he had a blast. We often look around as we get on a bus or at the airports and say, "Has there been a Rufus sighting?"

The Sooners had an interesting season in 2015. A Baylor assistant coach, Jeff Lebby, was on the Tulsa sidelines during the Tulsa—OU Game. The Sooners won the game 52-38 and Tulsa had a former long-time Baylor assistant as its new coach, Phillip Montgomery. Lebby was an OU graduate (2007) who had come to Norman to attend a wedding, and then went down to be with his old coaching friend on the Tulsa sideline.

Jeff Lebby had been a student assistant at OU due to a career ending injury in his freshman year, and Coach Stoops kept him on scholarship. Lebby later became a Baylor running backs coach, and later married Baylor coach Art Briles' daughter.

The NCAA or Big XII suspended him from his coaching duties the first half of the Baylor/OU game later in the year. It apparently was a scouting error that was frowned upon. Teddy said Lebby did not know he was doing anything wrong. Coach said, "Heck we did it all the time in earlier years." Coach Merv was an in-person scout in his first year as a Missouri assistant.

Later in 2015, OU took back the Big XII mantle from Baylor in Waco 44-34. It was a Game Day Saturday night slugfest and the Sooners held off the Bears. It was the third year in a row Baylor was higher ranked than the Sooners and the Big Red was a 2.5-point underdog. The Sooners ended the Bears undefeated season.

It appears that Lebby did not help them overcome the seven-point halftime deficit. I remember seeing him in the press box and saw him literally running down the hall during the half time break. I mentioned seeing him run to Coach Merv and he said, "I bet he was sort of embarrassed about all that stuff."

Sooners made the College Playoff in 2015

and played Clemson in the Orange Bowl. It was a tough game, and the Sooners led the game 17-16 at the half. Baker tried his best but could not connect with Mark Andrews and Sterling Shepherd in the second half (as he did in the first half) and we lost 38-17. We were shut out by Clemson and Brent Venables' defense. Sooners scored zero in the second half. I never thought I would see that. The Clemson game was one of only two games as a Sooner where Baker threw over 40 passes.

I remember how all the Sooner coaches congratulated Brent after the game. They still loved him after all the years and were genuinely happy for him. Coach said it was "impressive what Brent did, we did not expect those adjustments in the second half."

The Orange Bowl booth for the radio crew was so small and was virtually in the corner of the end zone and not high up. Coach said, "Do not know how Michael can get all his wires and stuff in there. It was like putting five guys in a broom closet." I laugh when I see Dolphin games and think of how little the space is in there with all the guys having to squeeze in.

We rode with Coach Merv (Tom Shores and I) to the TCU game in 2016. He was so interesting and fun to go with. Somehow, Coach was left off the team bus, and plane, but he was happy not to fly and do all the bus riding. We were honored to go with him.

It was a great TCU game, with Baker Mayfield and De De Westbrook having big games versus the Frogs, as OU came back from a 21-7 deficit. Coach was as excited as we were. It took us over an hour to find our way through the construction on the way home, and Coach was leading us all around Ft. Worth on roads he remembered from his Arkansas days, I am sure. Tom Shores was lost as well, and it took what seemed like forever to go about five miles to get on I-35. It was a fun trip. Riding with a true legend is always good. The extra couple of hours was worth it.

Merv (Mervin Lewis Johnson), said he grew up about 10 miles down a dirt road from King City, MO and played in the second football game he ever saw. He was big for his age and asked to play and they said, "why not." He had real problems with the athletic supporter because he had never seen one and it was not something you could, "just ask someone how they work." His folks, Mae and Claude Johnson, did not have a television and only had a radio, lived ten miles from town, and owned only one vehicle, so the family never knew what football really was, much less the equipment.

He was recruited to Mizzou by the legendary

coach Don Faurot. "I think somebody else came to sign me, but we drove down 200 miles to actually see the campus and to seal the deal." Merv also said that Iowa and Kansas offered him scholarships. "My high school only had seven points scored on us my senior year, and I made All Everything." His team won state and Merv made a name for himself as a football player. Merv was a good student and thus went off to the University of Missouri.

Merv was so poor that he even stayed on campus for Thanksgiving and only returned at the end of semesters. Coach said he was closer to Iowa State and even Nebraska than Columbia, MO. However, it was his state's university.

Coach talked freely about the first time he saw Kansas University basketball star Wilt Chamberlain as a student at Missouri. It was at Mizzou and the crowd was fired up and Kansas was obviously the favorite. He said, "Mizzou had a good post guy who was well over six foot, but looked small, compared to the 7'1" Wilt."

"The Tiger took the first two possessions for Missouri and took it right to Wilt and scored easy. This made old Wilt mad, and he dominated him from then on. He was something to see."

Merv Johnson played for Don Faurot until his senior year when he retired. He was the man who changed his life and gave him a chance to go to college. "I liked Coach Faurot," Coach quipped. No one in his family had ever gone to college.

Coach in his Mizzou Number 77 he wore in 1955-57

"I was on the last team that OU beat, number 47. They lost the next week to Notre Dame. Their second unit was so good, you never had a break. Teams went both ways, and they kept coming. They wore us out." Mizzou lost 39-14 at Columbia in 1957. (Mizzou was 19th ranked at that time.)

"That Tommy McDonald was so tough, and he would get hit, jump back up, and be ready to go again. He set the tone."

Coach then had Frank Broyles as his coach for his senior year. He completed his degree in four years, majoring in General Agriculture. He said that a degree in that was worth "nothing." He thought he might become a veterinarian, but Broyles really changed his life forever. Dan Devine took over at Mizzou after Merv graduated, but Coach did not really know Devine, as he was an Arizona State guy.

Broyles left Mizzou after one year for Arkansas. He later called Merv and asked him if he could come down and be a dorm guy and a freshman coach. Merv said that he must have, "seen something in him that indicated that he could be a coach."

Merv then went to Arkansas as a single guy. The actual coach of the Frosh was a track guy, who "didn't know anything he was doing" Merv quipped. After a couple of weeks, he was virtually the coach, and he stayed there for two years. Coach said it gave him a chance to see all the various positions and to learn them on the fly, offense as well as defense. He also was the dorm guy and responsible for keeping the boys in line. "Barry Switzer was one of them, so you know how that went," Coach laughed.

After two years living in the dorm while coaching the Arkansas freshmen, Dan Devine called him and asked him to come to his alma mater and help coach. So, he went to become a full time Division

1 assistant football coach at the University of Missouri at age 23. He finished his stint at Arkansas, went to the US Army (was a ROTC guy) and just got out of the service in time for fall practice.

The 1960 Missouri team, which was Coach's first year as an assistant, lost only one game, to Kansas — and "Kansas had an ineligible player and later had to forfeit." It was one of Missouri's finest teams and the loss to KU killed their National Championship hopes.

Coach said, "Someone asked Don Faurot if Kansas was known to cheat?" He said, "They got Wilt Chamberlain, didn't they?" It was obvious that Coach and the Mizzou staff thought Kansas had recruiting issues in football and basketball.

Mizzou officially went 11-0 but lost to KU 23-7. He laughed, "We beat OU that year in Norman for their first conference home loss in a long time (actually since 1942)."

"We went to the Orange Bowl and beat Navy and the Heisman Trophy winner. We held him (Joe Bellinio) to four yards. We did not win the national championship since Minnesota won their game and beat us out. President Kennedy was there at the Orange Bowl."

Coach was at games where President Nixon was (Arkansas vs. Texas in 1969), and the Orange bowl vs Navy with President Kennedy in attendance. He shrugged it off like it was not much. He was "too busy to think about that."

It was so fun hearing Coach relive these memories. It was like a window to the past had been opened and we got to peek inside. Coach also told us that he went back to Arkansas, got married, started a family, and embarked on another fun ride. When we arrived in Norman, he said, "We'll go over that on another day." What a trip and another Sooner win.

4. A Kid From Weatherford, Ok

Well, here I am. I am letting you know how lucky I am to be a part of such a talented group, and a great University. I found it amazing. Here is some stuff about me, the author. My actual name is Dennis G. Kelly, Jr.

I went to first grade in Austin, Texas and moved with my mother (I am an only child) late in that school year to Mangum, Oklahoma where my grandparents lived when my father passed away in March of 1961. My grandparents, Kelley and Grace Bowen, had a profound influence on me that is prevalent even today.

I finished the first grade and went to the second through fourth grades at Edison Elementary in Mangum. I got the opportunity to live with my cousin, Kel Bowen. He is five years older and introduced me to many sports, especially baseball and football. I also am probably one of the only lifelong

Sooner fans that lived in Stillwater, OK and Austin, TX. Both done before I was six years old.

Later, after my fourth-grade year, Mom, Jimmie Ruth Kelly, and I moved to Weatherford, Oklahoma in the summer of 1964. She finished college in Weatherford, and then attained a teaching job there.

My dad (Dennis, Sr.) was one of those guys who gravitated to Norman, Oklahoma after spending years with the Marine Corps in World War II. He was originally from Carter, Oklahoma and was a veteran of battles in Okinawa, the South Pacific, and Japan. He was not a football guy, but he loved it as a sport, along with baseball. In his prized possessions were pictures of the 1946 version of Owen Field and of the baseball stadium. He found his way to Norman, like hundreds of service men, and briefly attended OU. He loved the Sooners, Bud Wilkinson, and the Sooner football team.

I had found my dad's discharge papers in late 2010, and it said he took part in the engagement with Japanese Forces on Okinawa as well as in Japan. I asked my mom, shortly before her passing, and she had no knowledge that he was ever on the Island of Okinawa, part of the Ryukyu Islands off the south of Japan. He was one of the Greatest Generation that suffered in silence. I knew he did not like guns, and we never had one (other than a captured and partially dismantled Japanese rifle), and was adamant about not hunting. He never took part in family hunting outings and was often alone when the men went off with the guns and dogs. Dad survived a sniper attack while souvenir hunting in Japan after the war was over, so he felt blessed to even be alive.

He later returned to Sayre, Oklahoma (where I was born), where he met my mom, and they were married in late 1947. At the time of his death in March of 1961, we were living in Austin, TX (go figure). He was working as a controller and accountant. My dad died of a massive heart attack while (unbeknownst to me for years) we were conversing. I was his only son, and I have no other siblings.

It was a wonderful place to grow up, and Weatherford was always changing, challenging, a small college town, and was not too big to walk safely on the streets. I played sports all my years in Weatherford with a core of friends that were good athletically and academically. My lifelong friend, Larry Adler who I met on the day I moved to town. He loves the Sooners and Yankees and we talked then and now about them incessantly. No one knows more info stats and historic information by memory about them than Larry Adler. No one.

Our group of teammates, Larry Adler, Gary Amen, Gary Crissman, Floyd Adler, Mike Smith,

Lamont S. Woody, Mark Rowland, Jim Johnston, Dwight Holcomb, Ernest "Tubbs" Hubert, and Danny and Charles Killman had incredible success in all sports, particularly baseball. We won a state title in summer baseball for the 13-14 age classification in 1968, and we took part in State baseball high school tournaments. We did not lose a basketball game in grades seventh to ninth.

I came out pretty unscathed injury wise. I had a few broken noses and took a line drive in the left shoulder while pitching batting practice to our All-State Catcher Mike "Smazel" Smith. My teammates and coaches thought I was dead, but no.

The amazing thing was I only started **one game (1)** as a member of a WHS powerhouse baseball team. I was a bench player and keeper of the book. I was still so proud to ever start any game with such a tradition rich baseball program that included Ron Shotts, Charles Teasley, Mark Lumpkin, Steve Shotts, Stan Templeton, Roy Resler, Frank Sikes, Dom Garrison, Lawane Woody, Bobby Bailey, Mike "the Mayor" Brown, Clay Bruner, Todd Franz, Don Regier, Dillon Overton, Colby Miller, Jake Barrios, and all the greats that have and will follow.

One of the real problems I encountered as an only child without a father in the 60's and 70's was the inevitable question everyone asked, "Who is your daddy?" I always tried to avoid that question to the point of hiding and trying to avoid my friends' parents. It made me uncomfortable, and I really do not know why. I visited with Coach about it one Saturday and he told me, "It is hard growing up with a full family, much less alone or without a father. That happens to many of our players, it is tough." The Sooners often have players with single parents. Coach was right. It is tough.

*1968 Weatherford Eagles State Champion 13–
14 Year Old Preps Baseball Team*

My home was a "Christian" home, and I attended church and read the Bible. I was not much of a Bible student and really did not retain any of it. I just knew that the Bible was the inspired word of God, and my mother espoused it often. In my young life, I was mad that my earthly father passed away. It left me bitter, and I was not as receptive to Christian thinking as I should have been.

There was a period in the early 70's when there were numerous "Jesus Freaks" around. I associated with them, wore a cross and was comfortable being with them, but was a really just a putz. The people were nice to be around, the camps were fun, and there were a lot of pretty girls in church.

I did enjoy English classes in high school and in particular Miss Maureen Stuckey's class. We read many classic books and she drove the writing idea of clear and concise into my psyche. Coupled with Mrs. Betty Novak's speech classes, I was well prepared for college in the language and speech areas. Both boded me well. The only academic award I ever received was the Speech Award as a senior.

I was so fortunate to grow up and live in Weatherford, somehow God allowed me to be exposed to so many Godly people and I will be forever grateful for my time there. I was the chief of sinners like Paul espoused in 1 Timothy 1:15 and was blessed.

Our high school Weatherford team lost in the semi-finals of the state baseball tournament in 1971. We did, however, get to stay overnight in Oklahoma City, which was a real treat, reserved only for State qualifiers. We were staying at the

Holiday Inn West, just off I-40 and Meridian, and we got to eat at the restaurant, which was a real treat. I remember we were told to eat breakfast on $1.25 if we could. It was a real struggle.

After breakfast, just before we boarded the bus back to Weatherford, we saw Bud Wilkinson in the lobby of the motel. He said, "Hello boys," in that distinctive voice we all knew. We all spoke to him, and he could not have been nicer. Somehow the trip for me at least was worthwhile. We had crossed paths with a legend. Later, when I relayed this story to Coach Merv, he said he treated him the same.

I guess my interest in stats came in Weatherford as a young guy. I always kept a score while listening to baseball games on the radio. I also kept the scorebook for the high school baseball team when I was in only the seventh grade and up. I can recall going to tell the legendary high school Coach Doyle Bergner (in the 3rd base box) that I had to go home since my mom was there to pick me up, as they were playing in a big game with El Reno, OK. Weatherford baseball in high school was exceptionally good and they were almost always in the State Tournament.

I was a big Mickey Mantle and Roger Maris fan and followed the New York Yankees every day. I collected baseball cards and still have almost all of them. I read the stats on the backs of the cards and spent virtually hours reading the sports pages in the morning paper, The Daily Oklahoman each day. I also consistently read Sports Illustrated, Sport Magazine, and the Sporting News. I enjoyed the numbers and could not get enough. I saved my money and bought a Sport Illustrated subscription, eagerly awaiting each week's cover picture.

I always took pride in knowing that Mantle and Maris were both recruited to play football for the Sooners. The story of Roger Maris arriving in Oklahoma City bus station, turning around, and heading back to North Dakota was a circulated myth. I later learned that he had been on the OU campus for ten days or so and went home due to homesickness. Mantle never got that far. Both guys signed pro baseball contracts and the rest, as they say, is history.

I always had stats or record books around. I remember my first days doing the stats for the radio team. I would pack up all my reference material, and baseball style caps or hats I wear after the OU games. Coach Merv would always chuckle at me and give me that wry smile. He said, "I get a kick out of watching you pack," as we sat there late after the crowds were long gone.

I always wear a variety of different OU hats at each game. With each hat I wear, I try to change

the luck or karma for the team. The better the opponent, the more hats I bring. It can be from usually a three-hat team to a six- or maybe seven-hat
opponent. Coach loves it, as does Toby. I have done
stuff like that for most of my life. (I occasionally
work in a Yankee cap or Thunder for a change.)
Later, with the radio group, I tacked them up in
the booth and changed them during the game. One
great play hat or cap may come back into favor later
in the contest. Just fun stuff. It is not that I am superstitious, I am just cautious.

My first recollection of OU football was the
big win in 1963 against USC 17-12 in the LA
Coliseum. I remember they said it was well over
100 degrees (125 on the field at times), and Bud
Wilkinson was in his white short sleeved shirt and
tie-on TV.

By the time I recollect my first real college game
in 1963, Merv Johnson was a full-time assistant at
Arkansas and was in his fourth year of filling that
role. He had already been an assistant at Missouri
and Arkansas and was only 27 years old.

I went to my first live OU game in 1967. It was
9th ranked Colorado coming to Norman and Ron
Shotts, a Sooner player from Weatherford got us
the tickets. I went with my friend, Kim Arney, and
his mom and dad. Kim's dad Sid (C. C.) was an
OU law graduate and loved the Sooners. He would

clap his hands as he drove down the road singing Boomer Sooner. He always wanted us boys to love them too.

Ron Shotts was a Weatherford football hero (basketball and baseball too) and had been recruited by Bud Wilkinson to play for OU. He played for Gomer Jones, Jim Mackenzie, and Chuck Fairbanks (freshmen could not play) but due to Bud's retirement never played for him. He was a halfback that was 6'0" 195 pounds and he ran the hundred in 9.5 in high school. Kids in western Oklahoma rarely do that today, much less in the early 1960's. He was an Academic All American while at OU, drafted by the Dallas Cowboys, was an All-State halfback, served in the legislature, and later ran for Governor of Oklahoma.

Mr. Arney would often tell us about going to OU law school and how he and his brother, John, would share books. They did not have the money to buy two sets, so they took all the same classes. That always impressed me. They both became successful law partners, having their own firm.

Sid Arney was an enormous influence on me. He took his son Kim and me to our first OU game, and my first Major League baseball game in St. Louis (Cardinals vs. Reds). He never asked for any money, though I did not have any.

The Sooners won 23-0 vs Colorado and

All-American nose guard, Granville Liggins, made a virtual one-man goal line stand from the one-yard line that I will never forget. We sat in the north end zone, about halfway up as Granville was virtually making tackles all over the field. Ron Shotts had a great game, as did Steve Owens, Bobby Warmack, and Eddie Hinton. Ron got a great ovation as he came out of the game on a drive late in the contest. Steve Owens scored two touchdowns and Eddie Hinton added one rushing. The traffic was so heavy down Lindsey Street. I had never seen so many cars. Little would I know that would never change.

I inherited some pictures my dad had taken in Norman and OU in 1946. Those are treasured memories and I still look at and cherish them. They included Owen Field, tennis courts, baseball field and one of my dad at the entrance of the university. I was lucky to see all the places in person at my first game.

I now often before games go down on the field and look up at the section of my first seat. Greg Blackwood, Tom Shores, and I walk around Owen Field before (and the opponents too) almost every game, thinking and reflecting on the privilege. I even go up there and sit occasionally. I thank God every day for my life and for making me a Sooner. I have been so blessed.

The turf at Owen Field is managed by my

friend Jason Faries. One of the few all natural college football turfs in America is used so much, often painted, and basically tortured. Jason does such a great job with his crew and makes sure the turf is never a factor in any game, whether rain or shine. I appreciate him letting me walk on it before virtually every home game.

I can still list all the starters on offense and defense of the Sooners that played that day in November 1967. That team went on to win the 1968 Orange Bowl versus Tennessee.

The 1968 Orange Bowl was the only bowl game where Steve Owens scored a touchdown—a one yard run. Owens finished his career with 57 touchdowns. (Owens passed for a touchdown in the 1968 Astro-Bluebonnet Bowl). That Orange Bowl was also a showdown of the Sooners Granville Liggins and Tennessee's All-American Center Bob Johnson. By the second half, the Volunteers had to double team Granville. (Interesting stat for Steve, he threw for a couple of touchdowns, ran for 57, but never had a receiving touchdown).

Ron Shotts was the man when I was growing up. We kids would often go to his house when he was home from OU and wait around to see if we could yell, "Hello Ron" to him. He would say, "Hello boys." He always talked to us and made us feel important. He is a big reason I became a Sooner fan, an accountant, and an OU alum. I followed the Sooners every move, and still do.

Ron Shotts in his famous 22 for the Sooners.
The Weatherford, Oklahoma hero.

I was in the band all through school, from fifth

grade on. Weatherford was the kind of place where you could be in the band and still play sports. I played clarinet first and then switched to bass or tuba in the eighth grade. I was not particularly good but was part of a good band program in Weatherford. (I played bass drum in eighth grade as I ended my football season with a broken left arm doing the "Oklahoma" drill. I am still mad at the guy who hit me.)

My sophomore year I was in the marching band, and our band was selected to go to the OU Band Day and march on Owen Field. The Sooners played Iowa State that day in the fall of 1969, and my friend, Larry Adler and I were giddy with the chance to be on Owen Field. We hated band but would not have missed the opportunity.

It was quite an experience. We (high school bands and the Pride) made a huge map of the US, and I stood down on the 40-45-yard line. I still have a clipping from the Sunday Oklahoman the next day. It was also the only time in band that I ever told Dave Hanson what to do. Dave was a star band member, plays about 12 instruments, and has won so many awards, a jazz all-star, music professor, a true musician. I jerked him by the arm and put him in the right spot.

Steve Owens carried the ball for a still Owen Field record 53 times as the Sooners topped Iowa

State on that Band Day, on his way to the Heisman Trophy. What a day. Larry and I were so happy.

I also distinctly remember the Arkansas-Texas Game of the Century in 1969. Little did I know that I would become friends and lucky enough to spend time with one of the key coaches in that matchup.

I was rooting for Arkansas, and when I talked with Coach about it, "We thought we had them — that one was tough to take. That pass was a back breaker." Any time University of Texas wins anything, it is a back breaker in my books.

My senior year at Weatherford High School, I was lucky enough to go to the "Freedom Forum" at the Civic Center in Oklahoma City. It was great, there were patriotic speeches, highlighted by a speech by Jessie Owens, the 1936 Olympic Champion.

During the break of the speeches, we all went out into the lobby and there happened to be a box office for the Fullerton Ticket Agency. They had all kinds of concert tickets and a sign for Oklahoma football tickets. My friend Larry and I got excited and thought about Nebraska tickets (soon to be The Game of the Century in 1971) which was upcoming in a couple of months.

I hurriedly bought two tickets to "the game of the century" and had them in my hands. Larry was reluctant, said he would have to buy four or six due to family visitors on Thanksgiving Day, and passed on the purchase. I then at once had buyer's remorse.

I remember thinking...how was I going to get to Norman? Would my car make it, and the planning was just heavy. I sadly went back to the window and the nice lady gave me my money back. If I remember it was about $12. It was all the money I had. I got ever so close and will never forget it. Larry and I have talked about it often over the years.

WKY TV, later KTVY Channel 4, had been the exclusive home to the "Bud Wilkinson" show, the first ever college coaches show, and later the Jim Mackenzie, Chuck Fairbanks, and the Barry Switzer Show on Thursday nights. The show covered the Sooners and supplied the most up-to-date information you could find about the great OU program. (There were two shows originally, one for thirty minutes on a weeknight, and a playback show of the entire game for one hour on Sunday evenings following that week's game. They got combined into only a one hour "Coaches Show" in the 1990's.)

I think back often of trying to say the first phrase of each show "It's great to be back with you to talk about OU Football." Jim Mackenzie, Chuck, and Barry all said that, and Howard Neumann (none of us kids ever could find out where this guy came from) was always the host. My friends at school also watched the show each week, and we all commented on the guests and highlights. It was the only true look inside the program available.

The OU Coaches show had interviews, drawn up plays, replays of important parts of the previous week's games, and features. I do remember when Ron Shotts and Granville Liggins had a segment showing a 40-yard dash race. They both started out neck and neck showing the quickness of Granville, then the final few yards, Ron pulled away. It made an impression on me, and us kids, they were my heroes. I remember Jim Mackenzie was so impressed with those two (Little did I know that someday I would be sitting alongside Mackenzie's roommate on the road as they worked as Arkansas assistants).

In 1972, I bought a portable RCA Color TV, from Mr. Kissler at his RCA TV store, and "paid it out". I did this so I could watch the Chuck Fairbanks and Barry Switzer show from my bedroom. It was my first real credit purchase (about $279) to date, and I never missed an airing, or thankfully, a payment. That TV weighed about 60-70 pounds and was hard to carry and was anything but portable. I do remember Mr. Dawson at the Security State Bank (who made me my $279 loan) talking about paying your debts like in the Bible (Romans 13:8).

I decided late in high school to major in accounting. My father had been an accountant and had wanted to be a Certified Public Accountant (CPA) upon his death when I was six. My childhood hero, OU player Ron Shotts, had also majored in accounting at OU before getting a legal degree. I can still remember seeing in the Program (I still have) from my first OU game (vs. Colorado) that Ron's major was accounting. If it was good enough for Ron, I thought, then it was good enough for me. I lived at home and went to college in my hometown, majoring in accounting.

I really did not know what I wanted as far as jobs were concerned. The trend at the time of graduation in the 70's, was Oil and Gas, but for me it had no appeal. I sent out hundreds of resumes and had all types of interviews with all kinds of industries, but no offers. I was an average student with barely a three point GPA, but proudly worked my way through school. I was a janitor and worked at the local grade school. I also purchased a nice car.

Late in February of my final semester of college at Southwestern State, I saw a small chalk scribbled note on a blackboard which said, "The Oklahoma Publishing Company needs an Internal Auditor" and an address, etc. I responded to the inquiry via mail and sent a resume and was hired.

I graduated from Southwestern Oklahoma State in Weatherford, in May of 1976, with a BS in Accounting. I got an education for less than $2,000, had a paid for 1973 Olds Cutlass, $300, and no debt. I then moved to the Oklahoma City area. (I later attained an MA in Leadership from the University of Oklahoma. I used the hours of OU classwork I applied to my Continuing Professional Education (CPE) to keep my CPA license to get my master's and reach a lifelong dream of being an OU graduate.)

The Oklahoma Publishing Company (OPUB-CO) in Oklahoma City owned newspapers, the Daily and Sunday Oklahoman, a trucking company, a graphics company, a packaging company, as well as seven television stations and three radio stations. (They also had aired the OU Coaches shows.) Thus began my journey into the media and an exciting career as a Television Broadcaster.

I initially lived in Yukon, Oklahoma from 1976-79. I can remember the first year I was in the Oklahoma City area and going by myself down to Norman to see the reigning two-time National Champs play the University of California and their great All American QB Joe Roth. I could not miss a big Sooner game if I virtually lived in the same town. I only had $20 to last until payday (I only made $210 per week) and hoped to get in the game for $10. I always tried to go to big games over the years.

I tried desperately to buy a ticket as I stood outside the Stadium on the north side, just south of the Field House. I ran into one of my old Weatherford classmates that was going to OU to become a medical doctor, Mike Hall, and his wife Cassie. They were on their way to the game, and we talked. I have not seen either of them again that I can recall.

I could find tickets for $20 or higher, but I hated to take all the money I had until the next pay day. I left without seeing the game and drove back to Yukon and listened to the game on the radio. The Sooners held off Roth and I remember Switzer complimenting him and saying it was one of the "the greatest I have seen as a coach."

The Sooners won 28-17 and Roth then died soon of cancer. It was one of the first of the legendary visits to the opponent's locker room to compliment the opponents that Switzer made famous. I would have never dreamed as I drove back to my apartment in Yukon that one day I would be at every game and would sit virtually at the 40-yard line or better for free. I would have great parking and get to stay with the team on the road, go to all major bowls, and get to spend virtually three and a half months with a talented group of guys.

One of my few encounters with the legendary

Edward L. Gaylord, President and Publisher of the Daily Oklahoman and Chairman of the Oklahoma Publishing Company (OPUBCO group), came in the break room of the 4th and Broadway headquarters.

As a young accountant and auditor on one of my first coffee breaks, I sat at a table near Mr. Gaylord and another group of newspaper executives. I remember overhearing Mr. Gaylord say in a very calm matter of fact manner, "Ron Shotts is a fine man and would make a good Governor." I remember my heart soared. He was right and it endeared him to me as he confirmed what I always knew about my Sooner hero.

I had been a long-time reader of the Daily Oklahoman. It was my sports guide and I remember looking at all the stats on Sunday mornings about the Sooners. I also remember the pictures which always had the name of the players and the famous "Kalsu OU or Shotts OU" tag lines for the players pictured. This created hours of enjoyment.

I do also remember a story that an Oklahoman reporter named Jack Taylor did on Barry Switzer, which was controversial, while I was working at OPUBCO. It was not favorable to Barry, and he cancelled his paper. I came across a copy of the refund check by chance as an auditor of the accounting records. It was strange to say the least, and sad.

I would not have been hired for many of my jobs without being a CPA. The certificate is often the price of entry for positions I have reached. It helps me with the numbers on my stat job, but I do more mental math in the stat position, and I have spent a career telling people to use a calculator and do not do mental math. I remember taking my CPA exam with Joe Wylie, the great OU back. I conversed with him briefly, and he was a smart guy. He beat me in getting it passed. I was working at Channel 4 when I passed the mammoth CPA exam. It was three days of torture. Coach said to me one day that accounting stuff has been good to you. He was right.

I had a long discussion with Coach Merv at one of the long waits at a road game about the CPA exam, and he said, "Anything hard makes you better, you should be proud." I treasured that thought.

Here was a guy who was a member of the Oklahoma Coaches Hall of Fame, had a National Football Foundation Integrity Award renamed for him, and winner of countless awards and accolades and was telling me to be proud of my one deal. Vintage Coach Merv Johnson.

Within a month of my hiring, I was in a television station doing a balance sheet and operational audit and I then spent most of my career in a TV station or near one. (Up until that time I had watched TV, owned one, but had no idea the intricacies of the business.) OPUBCO gave me incredible experience in all their diverse companies, especially their TV stations, of which I am forever grateful.

In my career, I worked for public companies, family-owned private companies, partnerships, and highly leveraged companies. All my jobs, though travel has at times been extensive, mostly have been based in Oklahoma. Sooner born, Sooner bred.

In 2001, I joined Griffin Communications, LLC as Corporate Controller. I was with Griffin until my retirement in 2019 and was eventually the Managing Director of Business. Our company (Griffin) owned four television stations (KWTV-News 9, KSBI, KOTV and KQCW), multiple digital sites, was a partner at the onset in Sooner Sports Properties, as well as a Radio Network and Tower company. All of their companies are based in Oklahoma. Station KWTV, a CBS affiliate, was housed within the Griffin Corporate office in Oklahoma City.

I met Toby Rowland soon after I came to Griffin Communications/KWTV, and he quickly became a friend. I went by the sports office over the next decade and talked about all kinds of sports with him. He, Chad McKee, Curtis Fitzpatrick, Stan Chase, and all the sports guys were great fun to converse about a variety of sports, especially Sooner football.

Dean Blevins was the Sports Director at KWTV/News 9. He and I always talked OU. Dean was also the host of my beloved long running Sooner Football coaches show. The same program I coveted in my youth. Often, I asked for the scoop on what the coaches said.

Blevins was the original Sooner Magic Quarterback at Oklahoma. A 1976 pass by Dean to help defeat Nebraska 20-17 on the day after Thanksgiving, is when the term **"Sooner Magic"** reportedly was born. His pass that set up the winning field goal at Ohio State in 1977 only helped secure his Sooner immortality. Both these plays were from a Quarterback that had lost his starting job and was coming off the bench for the Sooners.

"Deano" is still the last Sooner to letter in football and basketball. He lettered in 1975 in both sports. He was a Norman, OK high school legend in both sports and chose to come to Oklahoma over several basketball and football schools. He was a passing quarterback who elected his hometown's exclusively running offense. His brother Paul Blevins, also played for Coach Merv at Arkansas and was a member of the 1969 team that played in the big game vs. Texas.

Toby was a small college basketball player, I was

a small college graduate, and I had a wife working at a small college, Oklahoma Christian University. We visited often about the Sooner Basketball conference and our love for the fun of small college NAIA basketball in Oklahoma. His Southern Nazarene University team played epic games vs. the Oklahoma Christian Eagles.

I can remember taking my family on a tour of KWTV Channel 9, and we all went by the Sports office one Friday night. Toby was toiling away producing a 10 pm sportscast. He was so gracious to my wife, mother, and my three girls. He was a nice guy who did not have the time nor the need to be so accommodating and kind. I would later, of course, spend more time with him.

I did get Toby and News 9 in trouble while visiting him at the "Meet the Sooners" day in early August 2004. I asked Adrian Peterson for his autograph, which was a no-no for media representatives during the press meeting with the Sooner players. Toby was doing his radio show from the playing surface of Owen Field, and I was sitting with him and Stan Chase from News 9. Adrian walked by and I asked if he would sign my Sports Illustrated cover, which he cordially obliged. I only got one, I only wanted one autograph, but it was an apparent violation. It was witnessed by someone from OU's Sports Information staff.

Toby told the Sports Information guys I was not media, just a News 9 "Big Wig", but that did not appease them. He had to do some fast apologizing for my miscue as an unofficial "media guy" to save News 9 from being banned from interviews and access to players. It was my only time to ever be a "Big Wig" of any kind and seemed funny to me. I sure did not want to cause problems. We all laugh at that now, but it was serious stuff.

I got to experience leadership lessons early in my career and I decided there is a certain style that I wanted as a leader and manager. My style is to encourage, give the staff a chance to gain or lose, and do their best. The story of Coach Merv encouraging a player to try to block OU All American defensive lineman Cedric Jones in a practice is a perfect example.

Michael Thompson was a Sooner receiver from Oklahoma City and was struggling and having no success blocking in practice. Coach Merv stopped play and calmly told him to do his best, that "no one in American can block him," freed him up to let go, do his best, and give best effort. It is the epitome of leadership with positive reinforcement and is the classic coaching by the legendary Merv Johnson. Thompson was blocking Cedric Jones who would later be a first round NFL pick of the New York Giants.

Coach Merv was the great Godly man that I thought he was. Overlooked for the head coaching job at Oklahoma, he never wavered. He was the epitome of an encourager, diligent worker, and gentleman though been done so wrong. He never was spiteful and did not take the way of the world, though he lived in the world. He was self-disciplined and worked incredibly hard. He was a living example of 2nd Corinthians 10: 3-5.

I have found that you are only as good as your staff, and I have had a good one everywhere I have worked. I was fortunate to work for companies that valued my department and felt we were an asset. I studied Bud Wilkinson and his style of positive reinforcement, self-discipline, and hard work (like Coach Merv), and I tried emulating him. Both Bud and Merv also treated people the way they wanted to be treated and tried to instill the will to prepare. I hope I did that, I sure wanted that result.

Coach Merv with David Overstreet and
Forrest Valora ... coaching them up

5. My Life Changes For The Better

My spiritual life struggled when I moved to Yukon, OK and I was on a five-year journey of not attending church. I used Sundays as just another Saturday and wandered farther from any type of faith.

I later moved to Oklahoma City in 1979 and lived on North Meridian St. It was there that I began going to church again after a long hiatus and was baptized for the forgiveness of sins and became a Christian.

I was originally baptized as an eight-year-old as part of a Vacation Bible School. I always struggled with that decision due to my age. I remember the ladies at the Vacation Bible School enquired about who had previously been baptized. It seemed as if I was the only one who did not hold up my hand. I distinctly recalled they exclaimed, "We've got to talk to your family," and it became inevitable. I did it and really did not protest, especially when they asked me if "I loved Jesus?" I responded with an obvious "yes" answer. I had no better answer to that question, I really did, and had all my life. I then was baptized.

I did have to wait several days until the end of Vacation Bible School to be baptized. That had always bothered me as I read many times about Phillip and his baptizing the Ethiopian in Acts 8 and his urgency to be baptized. Why did I have to wait for days? I was doing it in obedience, I guessed, but not to attain eternal life, and certainly not to receive the Holy Spirit.

After lengthy Bible study, I confirmed my faith, ending years of concern, and was baptized for the forgiveness of my sins and was immersed in water by my friend, Ronnie White on July 20, 1980, at the Village Church of Christ in Oklahoma City. I vehemently held onto Acts 2:38, "repent and be baptized every one of you for the forgiveness of your sins and receive the gift of the Holy Spirit." I also believed Mark 16:16, "whoever believes and is baptized will be saved, but whoever does not believe will be condemned." That day I became a member of the Lord's church and received the Holy Spirit. I later also became a Deacon in 2003 for the Memorial Road Church of Christ. I have also baptized my daughters, my greatest honor. My wife and I have diligently prepared our family for the eternity in heaven.

Elaine Denson and I married on Christmas night, December 25, 1980. We were married in front of a sparse crowd at the Quail Springs Church of Christ in Oklahoma City. Elaine is also a CPA and is an Accounting Professor at Oklahoma Christian University. I met Elaine while working at OPUBCO in 1978, and we began dating in September 1979. Our first date was at Ken's Pizza (which is now gone). I can remember she teared up when the Sooners lost to Texas in 1979, 16-7 as we watched the game at her apartment. I knew she was a keeper. She is also smarter than me, and makes my life easier, for sure.

My wife is a true Christian. When I began dating her, I often asked, "Are you going to church every Sunday, Sunday night, and Wednesday?" She said yes, and if I wanted to hang around with her, I had to do the same. Something about consistently hearing the gospel will change your outlook and it saved my life.

I recall going to church with her and waiting for her in the foyer of the Village Church. A little lady named Johnnie Tarpley came to me and asked me if I was looking for someone. I said a girl friend of mine and I distinctly remember her saying, "those

Church of Christ girls can bring them in." No truer statement spoken.

Elaine really has an admiration for OU football (and all OU sports) and was a six on six basketball player from Stratford, OK. There would be no way for me to have a spouse that did not follow the Sooners and was willing to go to games with me. She and I have been to Rose, Orange, Cotton, Sugar, and Fiesta Bowls, Final 4's for men (1988 Championship game), and women, also. The OSU Ice bowl game in 1985, and one of our big dates was the 1980 Stanford game. It poured down rain as we saw John Elway demolish our Sooners 31-14. A true lifetime of love evolved despite the deluge of rain.

We worked to make our girls Sooner fans, but none of them went to OU. Kelsey, our youngest is a rabid fan and has been to games including the Rose, Orange, Sugar, and Cotton Bowls. Kelsey's husband, Brice Carter, is a Sooner fan as well. Our middle daughter, Allison, is an artist and a music teacher by trade and could care less. She is married to an engineer/finance guy, Ryan Harms, who manages the endowments for the Oklahoma State foundation. Oh, well. Elaine is also an incredible manager of finances, and she has helped our family immensely. We have been on the Dave Ramsey plan long before there was a Dave Ramsey plan.

The girls did give us five great grandchildren, Andrew, Griffin, Harper, Lylah, and Vivian.

Our oldest daughter Denise has Down's syndrome. She lives with us and does not really care about football or sports unless it messes up her channels on TV.

When Denise was born, we did not know she was a Down's child. The Sooners upset the heavily favored Horns days after her birth in 1982, 28-22 and it was one of the most wonderful feelings ever. Denise was such a beautiful baby, and we were elated about the win. Kelly Phelps, Wendell Ledbetter (two touchdowns) had the games of their lives and Marcus Dupree went 63 yards, and OU upset the Horns. Things were great since OU beat Texas, and we had a beautiful family. Reality was soon to arrive.

We were shocked a few days later when we were informed of Denise's mental retardation. Since that time, we have made our best efforts to provide opportunity and a great life for her. She was the only Down Syndrome baby at that time to leave Mercy Hospital that was not diagnosed as a Down's baby before leaving. They assessed her chromosomes and told us the tough news later. It was a devastating blow.

I have talked with Coach about her, and he calls her "your special person." I told him that the win in 1982 vs. Texas was one of the greatest wins ever — he liked it too. "We took it to them on that day," he said. Some solace for a tough time for my wife and me.

I always reflect on how we did against Texas in the years they were born. Denise and Allison were **both** born on September 29th, two years apart, and Kelsey was born on October 10. All of them around the Red River game date. We are 2-0-1: 1982, 28-22 win, 1984, 15-15 tie (ugh), and 1986, 44-9.

I have talked with Coach often about the 15-15 Texas game. He always says, "We had the ball on a fumble before the Stansbury play." I have watched the video often, Coach is right.

Coach lost his daughter, Jill Johnson Foster in a tragic car wreck in 2000. She was only 29 years old. He said to me one day that a parent should not bury a child. What a loss for him and his wife, and his encouraging words to me when we talk about my daughter is priceless. In about ten minutes with the guy, you feel better, inspired, and understand why he is loved. He encourages me with my daughter and the life with a perpetual eight-year-old.

6. Vintage Coach
And Memories

Coach Merv drove Tom Shores and me to the OU-TX game in 2016. He drove the opposite of his demeanor and we were scared all the way. Tom called it "Mr. Toad's wild ride." Coach talked about the last time he drove down there to the OU-TX game. I began thinking that he had done those two times in about the last 30-40 or so years, as we turned, raced, and sped through Dallas traffic. He had done it so many times in a charter bus but not in a car. Man were we on quite a trip.

Coach began talking about coaching with Howard Schellenberger. He said it was quite an adventure. He (Howard and his wife) would drive to games in his own car or a rented limo, which led the team buses. His wife would also roam the sideline and yell at the players, trying to fire them up. Many times, she was in an "expensive coat."

Coach said the staff meetings lasted about 20 minutes, which is the shortest of his career. He said Howard would come in and often yell at anyone that was late.

"He always lit into this young coach he brought with him to OU, but he was his favorite," Coach said.

He then would show this stack of pages in a bound book and say "These are the plays that won the National Championship when we beat Nebraska. We need to run them." And then the meeting would be over.

I asked Coach, "What did you do?"

Coach said, "We spent the rest of the day trying to figure out what it took to run the plays. Never talked about our players or needs."

Coach also said that Dr. Boren sent a guy around often to ask him about the safety of the players. Dr. Boren was worried, and Merv said, "I was too. It got bad." Howard was famous for not allowing the players to drink water around practices. A dangerous routine.

While on the ride to Dallas, Coach told us, "Doctor Boren told Joe C. he would like for Toby to be considered as the Voice of the Sooners and he should be on their list (of candidates). Joe C. heartily agreed." Off it went, with Coach one of Toby's biggest promoters and advocates.

This is a great example of the years of teamwork for Joe and Boren. They could have looked for a "national guy", but Joe agreed with Doc Boren, and they took a chance on a dark horse candidate with limited play by play experience. Like the chance they took when they put a coach (Coach Merv) in the press box adding color commentary, with virtually no experience, for one of the nation's elite teams and a massive radio audience. The Sooners are famous for selecting one off the staff or assistants for big jobs. Bud, Barry, and Bob to name a few.

I had asked Toby about his chances for the job before he was named the Voice, and he mentioned he did get to talk to Dr. Boren. He was as Toby said, "In his office when Henry Kissinger called for Dr. Boren." I was in such awe of that, and I remember thinking what a big-time opportunity for him.

I am positive the Sooners and Learfield originally had a short-term deal for Toby. Now it is a long-term deal. Great news for the Sooners and Sooner fans everywhere. I am sure that President Boren would never have selected a person that Joe was not comfortable with, and Joe would never have trusted the hearts and souls of the Sooner faithful to someone who could not deliver. Learfield and Sooner Sports Properties (their Oklahoma division) actually own the rights to the Sooner radio broadcasts and employ the radio personnel. However, the University has the ultimate say and approves the announcers that represent them.

Toby has been the voice of every major sporting event the Sooners have produced since 2011. He does football, men's basketball on radio, and sometimes women's basketball on TV, baseball, some gymnastics, and is one of the best emcees for Sooner caravans, banquets, rallies, and everywhere the Sooners need him. He is an amazing guy who works six to seven days a week for about 11 straight months. His position with OU was virtually the voice for everything that is OU. Toby had done basketball play by play, but had not really done football, but is a natural. His experience with News 9 and with Southern Nazarene University helped make it all click.

Toby is so creative and has a flair for new things and ideas. He coined the phrase "Palace on the Prairie" and invented the "scene setter" that Sooner fans wait for each week which sets the tone and the excitement for each week's game. He uses the term "Oh Mama" when the Sooners do something spectacular and his "You can unhitch the wagon and put the ponies in the barn" and "Win column Sooners" are the phrases that all of Sooner Land waits for, as it signals another Sooner victory in any sport! Toby Rowland is now a Sooner legend too. A nicer person cannot be found. A true gentleman, family man, Christian leader, and professional.

Coach, Tom Shores, Greg Blackwood, and I were chatting about the Sooner softball team in 2016. We were in the lobby of the hotel waiting to go to Reliant Stadium in Houston, TX for the season opener vs the University of Houston. We had just seen Patty Gasso in the lobby and said hello. She commented to me, "I like your 2016 National Championship Softball hat" that I was wearing.

Coach said, "That Patty (Gasso) is about the best coach on campus—may be the best that has ever been here in about any sport." I had to really sit down on that one. Here is a guy who played, coached, and or worked with Stoops, Switzer, Frank Broyles, Dan Devine, Don Faurot, Johnny Majors, Mack Brown, Jim Mackenzie among many—he should know coaching. What an endorsement!

(And just before this book was going to press, Patty Gasso and her 2023 Sooner softball team won their seventh national championship, three in a row, and are carrying over a 53-game undefeated winning streak into the 2024 season.)

After the Sooners beat Texas 45-40 in 2016, Coach drove us out of the Cotton Bowl parking lot, weaving, and passing cars in the wrong lane. We stopped at a light next to an expensive red Camaro.

The driver shot past us and really shot out of sight. "I think she was not really happy," Coach said. I could not help but laugh. Coach then shot across a parking lot, jumped a curb saying they will "let an old ball coach through." He gave the cars a gentle wave as we weaved out of the Cotton Bowl area.

We stopped in Denton, TX on the way home from the Sooner win and Coach got out of the car and left it in gear. Jumping over and stopping a car, even an idling one, is a problem. Coach had jumped out to give this homeless man some money, which is vintage Coach Merv. That was scary, but not as bad as when he took his hands off the wheel and put on his sunglasses as we rode through Jersey barriers at around 75 mph. It was something.

Later that season, Tom Shores asked Joe Washington if he had ever ridden with Coach. Joe looked at him scarily, like how did you survive. "You have?" Joe said. Joe emphasized that we better be careful.

Joe Washington, Sooner legend, stays at Merv's house for days each month. Coach said he "has so many deals going, and he has a business in Baltimore." Coach loves Joe and is happy to have him. I am sure he gets lonely.

"Joe is so much fun," Coach said. "I have these two cats and one of them is scared to death and will hide till Joe leaves and the other one loves him." He laughed at that one.

Coach had a couple of cats that are brothers, and they sat on the arms of his recliner as he watched TV—which was mostly football and mostly Sooner sporting events. I would have loved to see him sitting on his throne with a couple of cats, one on each arm. Coach says they would fight each day for about two to three minutes. Neither one hurts the other, but they roll around and look like they are going to kill one another, then they calm down and walk off. The Sooner football legend and his pussy cats.

The one game that most Sooners and Texas Tech folks will never forget was the 66-59 win at Tech in 2016. Mahomes versus Baker. OU had a 500-yard passer (Baker), 200-yard rusher (Joe Mixon) and 200 yards receiving (De De Westbrook). It was amazing, and it was another Sooner game that will live forever.

Teddy was distraught because of the 59 points and the defense let downs—no one could have stopped these two QB's on that day. Toby was so excited, and it was a virtual lifetime of offense, but the holes in the defense were clear. I wore out so many pencils, scanned my phone, and thumbed through the media guides and used all my references materials, it was wild. Records were broken by the minute.

We had to console Ted, he was so sad for the

defensive coaches and defense. It was really the high and low of this job. The players become so real, and we get to see them in all kinds of situations. The offense was so pumped and excited, and Jordan Evans and the defense were devastated, though getting the one stop they needed. The great fact is we won, and it was at Tech.

The duel between Baker and Tech's Patrick Mahomes was one that will be discussed forever. The two teams finished with each team having 854 total yards of offense. Mahomes had 734 yards passing and Baker had 545. An interesting stat was Baker threw 52 fewer passes than Mahomes. (He threw 36 to Mahomes' 88.) Everyone always thought Baker aired it out, but he only threw 40 or more passes two times at OU (Clemson and K State in 2017), that is two times in 40 games. (He threw 40 or more six of the eight games he played in at Tech.) He may be one of the most efficient passers ever.

Teddy was so worried about Mike Stoops, his old coach, and was really in a dilemma. We were winning, but not in a traditional Oklahoma defensive effort. When you score in seconds, the defense is always seemingly on the field. This became the new norm in the Lincoln Riley system. I was afraid we were morphing into another Texas Tech, and no one ultimately wanted that.

Coach Merv had been on the staff when the Sooners had **no pass attempts** in 1986 at Colorado (28-0 win). He was there when we had **no completions** in a 1989 loss to Arizona, a 6-3 loss that saw the Sooners go 0-4 in passing. He just shook his head and said to me, "If you live long enough, I guess you can say you have seen about everything. Times have sure changed." (By the way, Jamelle Hollieway threw only 56 passes in the Sooners 1985 National Championship season.)

In the 2016 Kansas game, a kid named Devin Montgomery scored a TD on his first carry ever at OU. We were talking and, in my notes, I had that there had been three others do it (that number has been since researched and there are more), Dale Crawford in 1950, Mike Thomas in 1972, and Darrell Shepherd (Sterling's uncle) in 1979. Coach piped up, "Doug Switzer (Barry's son) did it against Missouri in 1992 or so and it was a one-yard run." I did not have that nor did OU on their notes. I looked it up and Coach was right in that Doug scored a one-yard TD run on his first ever carry. Coach also could spot when the teams did not have eleven on the field. It was always a surprise when he would say "They have only 10 guys." It was incredible. He was always right.

Coach has impressive grandsons that were at OU. He was excited he would soon have five grand kids at OU. His daughter, Jan, and her husband were moving back to Norman and were building a new house just up the street from him. They all will get to again see the love the Sooner community has for him.

We all rode via cars to the stadium from the team hotel at Iowa State in 2016. Coach was in the lobby while we were all waiting and was reflecting on his offer to become the coach of the Cyclones. He said he turned it down and thought he was too young. That would have been in 1967, and he and Johnny Majors were assistants at Arkansas under Frank Broyles. Coach Merv turned it down and Majors got the job, and he was there from 1968-72.

He had told us about having an offer for the Wichita State job once. He said, "I am sure glad that I turned that down since they do not even have football now. They turned the school over to someone who did not see the value."

Michael Dean, OU's Producer Engineer, virtually ate up all the buffet food in sight at the Ankeny, Iowa Marriott. He said, "Since he won't have a chance to eat until late at night." We then all rode in cars to the Iowa State stadium. Ironically, as we walked to the Media and Press Gate at ISU's Jack Trice stadium, the gate was near the "Johnny Majors" parking lot. I pointed to the large sign remarking to Coach "Look Coach, you could have had your own lot." He chuckled and said, "Well, that may not have been too bad." We all laughed.

The whole crew flew to Morgantown to play West Virginia University in 2016. We all flew on the staff and "friends" plane that was smaller than the team plane and landed in a snowstorm. It snowed virtually the whole time we were in West Virginia. Coach was with the players and their flight.

I sat near Tim Lashar, the hero of Sooner games on the plane. I told him how I appreciated his Sooner career and in particular, the big kick vs O State in 1983, and I was there when he kicked four field goals vs. Penn State in the victorious 1986 Orange Bowl. Tim is truly genuine and a nice person. He appeared so appreciative of my memories. Coach told me later he was, "The best around, probably best ever at OU."

In Morgantown on one of our pregame visits, I lamented to Coach about my originating the term/slogan "4 Warn or Four Warn" for the weather acronym while working at Channel 4/KFOR-TV. It happened very impromptu in a management brainstorming in 1990 (that I only walked through) and said it out loud. I complained to him how it makes me "still cringe to hear it used." Coach said, "Life is like that, sometimes they take your stuff and run with it."

I felt like such a dunce. I had complained to the

one guy who had the OU head coaching job taken from him. I felt sad and a real sense of melancholy. I sure hope he forgot that snafu.

Sooners beat WVU as Sooners kicked off in the snow for the first time in 50 years. The guys jumped out early and held on for a 56-28 win.

We flew out of West Virginia in the snow, and I was so anxious to leave. I thought they would never quit de-icing the plane. It was the only time I can ever remember while flying that I was truly nervous. I noted to myself that Joe C, Toby, Rufus, Teddy, Joe Washington, Lashar, and a host of big names were on the plane, so it was probably safe.

I had physical problems getting around and walking in 2016 and it culminated in all the walking at the 2017 Sugar Bowl game in New Orleans. The Sooners played Auburn, and ironically it was Bob Stoops' last game, a big win over Auburn (of the SEC). Coach Merv said a couple of times, "You're really laboring" especially up and down the stairs, tripping a couple of times at the Super Dome. His comments made me think.

I came back that next week and started on a Weight Watchers' lifestyle that has helped me lose 50 pounds, and to date I have kept it off. Coach has a way of doing that to you when he talks to you in the firm concerned voice.

That Auburn game was the last game in the Stoops era. The Sooners soundly beat the Tigers in a great game. Little did we know that Bob would bow out and Lincoln Riley would be next. Coach said Lincoln was one of the "sharpest offensive minds" he had seen.

It was the final time to see Samaje Perine and Joe Mixon. They had been so productive and were especially nice kids. Joe Mixon never did not speak, and was a "Yes sir, kid." Coach liked him and said he had overcome "tough circumstances."

But Samaje was one for the ages. He left the Sooners as their all-time rushing leader and that covers guys like Owens, Sims, Pruitt, Little Joe, and Adrian. Think about that one. Coach said on our way home that he "came to the team ready to play and never stopped working." When Samaje Perine arrived in Norman, the new freshmen saw him from afar and they all asked, "Whose dad is that?" He was developed and had such a mature presence. Sooners were going to miss him, and I was so honored to see every snap he took.

Beginning in 2017, the Sooners added a Hispanic radio broadcast. Enrique Vasquez and Luis Rendon began traveling and working with us. They are great guys and have added another dimension for the Sooner radio fans for a growing Hispanic audience. The fun part is the places they have to do the games. Opponents are not set up for more radio personnel, so they are often on the roof, under a big umbrella and also get some really nice suites. Sooner opponents don't really want the regular radio deal to have any space, much less one more broadcast set up.

I was lucky enough to drive Coach to the OU/TX game on Friday before the 2017 game. It would be Coach's 56th time facing the Longhorns. I insisted on driving him, as the last time he drove was one that was truly frightening. He really wanted to drive, and he sensed that I really did not trust him. And he was right. He even tells people this and always laughs.

The OU/Texas game is always a logistical credential deal (we have to find someone who has them) and parking passes are scarce, thus a potential nightmare. Every year we come to the gate, often at 5 am in the morning preparing for an 11 am kick off, and the gate people do not want to give us entrance to the parking lot. Every year, "What are all these Oklahoma people doing here?" Duh, we have been doing this for about a hundred years at the fair. This questioning happens every year without fail. I love the game, but the Texas State Fair masses are no fun for me.

Coach was speaking to the Ft. Worth OU Alumni group this Friday in October 2017 before the OU TX game, and I was his "guest". He delighted the crowd at the largest building in Ft. Worth, and he was so gracious to all the attendees. So many people love him, and it is really something to see. His speech was just what the alums wanted, and I am sure they all sensed they were seeing a true Sooner legend. He even addressed his not being a "Head Coach" and his turning down offers, but that he made the right decision to be a lifetime Sooner. He makes you feel so good. He also reiterated that he had a "General Agriculture" degree that was worth nothing and the crowd roared. They all loved him. So many came and gave him all kinds of love and admiration.

Coach also introduced me, and said that I drove him down because, "I did not trust his driving." That brought another laugh. But it was true.

Berry Tramel of the Oklahoman said very complimentary things about Merv at the Ft. Worth Alumni gathering. I did not know at that time, but Berry gave a "state of the Sooners" analysis every year to the group.

Coach talked about his Arkansas team as we drove around Ft. Worth. He said they were a good team and had Jerry Jones and Jimmy Johnson on the team. He also said they really had no stars, just talented players. He was a roommate of fellow assistant, Jim Mackenzie on road games. "I woke up more than once thinking something was on fire and realized Jim had started smoking before he got up from the bed. Jim played for Coach Bryant at Kentucky (Beat OU in Sugar Bowl in 1951) and initially tried to be a tough guy but made a real change and became a player's coach. The players loved him.

Coach talked about the Texas game vs. Arkansas in 1964. He said, "That guy (Darrell Royal) said that Ken Hatfield would not get a punt run back or something like that. He was always saying things. Hatfield ran one back for about 81 yards, and he laughed. That was a heck of a game, 14-13, which held them off to have an undefeated season." Coach can remember the great details of a game. It was 81 yards, as I looked it up. (He always referred to Royal as that guy.)

Merv said that the Arkansas coaches used to play pickup basketball at noon. It was rough, and Mackenzie would always have to stop and lean on the wall out of breath, which would have been the prelude to heart problems that would take him by a heart attack in the spring of 1967.

Merv said he was hoping to succeed Broyles at Arkansas, but "Back in those days, Arkansas was having tough years and he (Broyles) was hoping to keep his job, and not worrying about him getting the job or who would be next." Coach said that

Broyles always said it is about character of the team and the fourth quarter. "Fourth quarter is what makes the difference." He was right.

He also told me of the Notre Dame job that Dan Devine had vacated after 1978. The Irish Athletic Director privately told Merv that they would like for him to be the coach, but that "Notre Dame would never turn it over to an assistant. Would only hire someone with head coaching experience." Their loss was OU's benefit as Coach then came to Oklahoma in 1979.

Barry Switzer had called Merv at Notre Dame in early 1979 with intentions of getting names of offensive line coaches in the country to replace one that left for the NFL. To Switzer's surprise, Merv said he was the best offensive line coach around, and the rest is OU history. Switzer never expected to get his old Arkansas friend for his O-line coach. Coach Merv said, "My wife and family did not like the wintry weather, but otherwise they loved South Bend. Oklahoma was further south and warmer." Our gain, Notre Dame nothing.

Coach said that Dan Devine was good to work for and gave him free reign. Devine did watch Monday Night Football games, and then come in all excited-on Tuesday's and tout trick plays he had seen and wanted to run. Coach said, "I would humor him, install something that did not work, and then basically do whatever I wanted offensively. Think we did it once or twice and that was it." He laughed at that one. When you have Joe Montana and that group, why not? Coach worked six years for Dan Devine with two years at Mizzou and four years at Notre Dame.

On September 17, 1966, over 50 years ago, the Sooners left the traditional white helmets with a single red stripe and numbers on each side (1957-1965). On that fateful Saturday, they debuted an all-red helmet with an interlocking white OU that is used today. The Sooners played Oregon on that 1966 Saturday. They beat Oregon, the team with current day multiple uniform changes, 17-0.

The red used in 1966 was closer to Arkansas red. Rumor has it that the Arkansas influence from Jim Mackenzie, hired off Arkansas' Frank Broyles's staff set the color. (The red was later changed to crimson in 1976.) When the Arkansas similarity of color was noticed in 1966, Arkansas was near a recent National Championship (1964), with Coach Merv on the staff and were atop the college football world. It was a good enough color then.

That September 17th also signified a change from the Jim Tatum, Bud Wilkinson, and Gomer Jones family era of coaches, and rang in the regime of a new coaching tree, the late Jim Mackenzie, Chuck Fairbanks, Barry Switzer, and of course,

Coach Merv. Thus, began the use of the easily recognizable helmets, with the OU on each side that is now world known.

I did befriend Rusty Weller, a student assistant at OU during 1966 in Harold Keith's Sports Information Department. Rusty told me he was there when Mr. Keith sent him with a note to Coach Mackenzie down on Owen field about the unveiling of the new 1966 helmets to the press, but I cannot find a follow up story—anywhere.

My researching the Daily Oklahoman archives about the helmet change and the famous inter-locking OU revealed nothing. The September 18, 1966, story about the game said nothing about any change in helmets. I looked at the final game in December of 1965 vs. Oklahoma State which showed the Wilkinson era white helmets (their last official use). I asked Coach about what he knew about the inter-locking OU and the red color. Did he know about it or someone who may have known? Who picked the OU inter-locking? Could I have just missed it in the archives?

Coach said, "Ask Switzer." I thought to myself, here is a guy who talks to Frank Broyles, Joe Washington, Joe Montana, Switzer, Larry Lacewell, Jerry Jones, the Selmons, who is going to take my call?

I did get to actually ask Barry near his house on a walk with Coach one afternoon. He said it was due to the new head coach and he really did not know. He said it was the "coaching change." Really, at that time, it was the first major change of Oklahoma coaches since 1946. I made inquiries with my friend Mike Brooks, Sooner historian who did not know. I guess as the stat information says in the weekly Sooner Game notes sometimes states, it is "under research". (If anyone reading this knows the answer to whose idea was the inter-locking OU, and the story, my publisher promised to add that info to this book in the next printing.)

Coach leading Tom Shores on a tour of the stadium in 2017. Coach was a tour guide for years at Owen Field. Best in Sooner history.

7. A New Era

We had a big win at Ohio State in 2017. OSU were favored in the odds, and Baker Mayfield had another of his great games. He planted the OU flag that day in the center of the Ohio Stadium and it was one of OU's greatest all-time wins, 31-16.

I was lucky enough to walk that turf of Ohio stadium earlier that game day during the team walk-thru. I scoured the surface where in 1977, the late Mike Babb recovered the big 4th quarter onside kick, where Dean Blevins passed for 17 yards to Steve Rhodes to set the spot where the winning 41-yard field goal by Uwe von Schamann was kicked. It is the ultimate example of Sooner Magic. The magic was continued over the Ohio field in 2017, same as forty years before.

Baker ended up apologizing and the flag planting controversy has gone on for years. It was the largest crowd to see a non-Michigan game at Ohio stadium (as of 2017). Coach had never been to the stadium before, and he was "impressed how we played, offense and defense, folks don't come in here and win very often." He says so much with few words.

Coach is so nice and got me tickets to the Ohio State game for my friend Sam Moore and his son Kyle. He got them because he is Merv Johnson. There were none to be found, and they were miraculously found for him at regular price. They were going for $500-$1000 for each ticket. He is the man at OU, and he has the golden touch, and it was appreciated. He does so many little things, (tickets, and tours) especially for former players, and they all love him. (I try not to bug him, he has so many that he helps.)

Tom Shores asked Coach if he could get us an autograph ball of the 2017 Sooners. He took a big bag of balls to the locker room and did it. Coach said, "I got all the players and not just trainers and guys who do not play." It is one of my prized possessions since it has Baker and Kyler. What a piece of memorabilia! It was so funny watching Coach carry this big bag of balls. He gave them to the game day security ladies—Janice and Shirley—in the press box as well. It was so Coach Merv like.

By the way, we get to stay at the team hotels on almost all our trips, and the accommodations are really first class. The Sooner team takes over a hotel in Ankeny, Iowa; Ft. Worth, Lubbock, Texas; (with the 10 Commandments out front). But the accommodations at the Bowl Games are incredible. The 4- or 5-star hotels and the services are amazing. I mean amazing; winning really pays!

The Sooners always get the other team's best shots, and it is amazing how many opposing fans yell at the team buses (some are just staff and trainers) as they pass. It is something to see people in Tallahassee do the tomahawk chop at about 8:00 in the morning or have the Ohio people shoot the finger at a bus that does not even have anything OU on it. Pretty funny to see. Many of the guys on the bus are trainers and staff folks, nothing even resembling a player.

Riding on the team buses for transport or travel from the various hotels is an incredible experience. Those police escorts are something one can really get accustomed to enjoying. I remember saying to T-Row at Ohio State, as we raced through Columbus, OH in 2017, "Do you think Rutgers gets this treatment?" T-Row said, "OU pays for this escort." What a deal. The Sooners are all first class, but poor Rutgers may walk.

The funniest things that sometimes happen on the air are the questions that Toby asks Coach. Toby tries to set him up for a question about a topic and then Coach goes into a great barrage of incredibly insightful analysis. However, with his poor hearing, he does not know we are not on the air. Toby says, "Say it just like that when we come back on the air." You cannot help but smile.

Coach got a new phone in 2017. He had one of the last flip phones ever and the Athletic Department got him a new I-phone. He did not really know how to use it and it had an alert tone. We were well into the first game and there were little faint dings going off. I know Coach could not hear it, and the producers at Learfield were asking what the tones were. Toby and Michael Dean were puzzled.

I hate to say it, but I knew where the tones originated. I finally got them turned off at around half time. I laughed often about it, as I was blaming Shores on the intercom that went over the headsets (the intercom is heard by the whole crew but is not heard by the listeners). Shores kept saying it was not him. He later said he knew I was jacking with him. I loved blaming Tom and Michael. It is so much fun.

Coach is a real radio warrior. He sits there for the whole game and does not generally get up at halftime. He does not drink much and can sit there for all game, which sometimes lasts more than three hours. He is amazing. However, on a couple of occasions he will just get up at the end of a quarter or half and take off, but he forgets to take off the headset. It is a real effort to catch him as he strings the cord to the limit. He said one time, "Heck, I forgot I was still hung up." Many times, Coach tries to make sure I have something to drink or eat during a game. He will sit there not eating or moving, but wants you to be ok.

Dr. Boren was a champion for Merv, Toby, Joe, and our broadcasts and is a leader I admire and love. There may be things that some people do not like about his style or even some of the results, but he is a master at relationships and the trivial things that make you comfortable. His kindness afforded to me is forever appreciated and the picture I took with him at Kansas in 2017 is a prized possession.

Coach invited me down to a practice in 2017. Tom Shores and I went and met Coach for a tour he gave us. He said, "No one does 'em anymore, so I guess I'll do them." It was first class, and he was so nice to us. He treated us like we were especially important, which he does for everybody.

We got to see his new office and take some pictures. He showed us his video set up and how he gets to review the games. He sat at his desk, turned it on, and started watching. He started analyzing some plays and remarking about some "guy out of position, and that was holding." It was a view of the true master with decades of knowledge and skill. I wanted to pinch myself.

We got to see the incredible outdoor facility, the locker rooms, and all the trophies. Coach went by the scale in the weight area and stepped on it. "Still at my playing weight—217-18," as he popped on the scale. He was proud. Not many can say that after about 60 years since his last snap.

Everyone down there loves him, and I mean players, coaches, and staff. They all go out of their way to say—"Hey Merv." He acknowledges them, and he walks all over the place. Security clearances do not mean a thing since he "owns" the Switzer Center.

We stood on the sidelines during practice, and he studied several of the plays. He would point out numbers (as he does not remember names very well anymore). "Watch that 6" he would say as Baker would thread the needle to someone. It was this guy this and this guy that. It was an analysis with an all timer. It was one of the greatest highlights as a Sooner fan I have ever had. I also got a picture of Coach in a hat since he almost never wears one. One guy he really liked was number "81", now that guy may be our best overall player. He was talking about Braden Willis who later changed to number "9". He really did become a clutch player. A true star in 2022.

I ate with coach at the team training table of the Renaissance Motel on the night before the TX game in 2017, what a spread. The team buffet is something to behold. Soup, steaks, fruits, desserts, all kinds of stuff in incredible amounts. "No need to just throw it out, it's so much food," coach quipped. It was AMAZING, almost sinful, it is so abundant.

The radio crew were in the lobby of the motel in Temple, TX, preparing to go to the Baylor game in 2017. We were driving to the game and the parking passes were handed out to the guys who had driven down. Tom Shores casually asked Coach if the "Switzer Wine" store on Lindsey was owned by Coach Switzer. He said well "Shoot yes, it's got his name on it." We all roared.

Coach was talking to a guy in the lobby of the motel. He was an incredibly large man and was so respectful of Merv. Coach gave him a couple of tickets and he left.

I asked coach who that was. Oh, he was "an old lineman for OU before I got here." It was OU's Outland Trophy winner Greg Roberts. My mouth dropped open. Coach hob nobs with all the greats and they are all players to him, and they all love him. I guess when you hang around Billy Sims, Joe Montana, Baker, Jason and all those guys, a mere "lineman" is just another guy.

We lost a heartbreaker to Iowa State in 2017.

The Sooners lost 38-31 and they (ISU) were much better than expected. It was the only regular season Big 12 loss of the year.

Coach had said that Iowa State was good. Fundamentally sound and fierce tacklers. He mentioned before the game that they tackled by diving low and "cutting the legs" out from under ball carriers.

Abdul Adams had an all-time Sooner record 99-yard run vs. Baylor, finished with 164 yards, and had 42 yards on three carries vs. ISU. They cut Abdul down at the ankles on a tackle, and thus ended his year.

Poor Abdul, he did not play again in 2017, and with the spectacular play and emergence of Rodney Anderson he decided to transfer to Syracuse. We all hated that Iowa State tackling was not illegal but was fierce. At least Abdul will have a record that will stand forever. It may be tied, but never beat.

Coach did come back the next week and said that Iowa State was holding on every play and by every offensive lineman. "Was the worst I had ever seen." Now that will get your attention. Coach really studies the video and does his homework.

He took me aside and showed me the moves they were using. You should have seen the legendary Coach Merv gripping me and moving me around. He had obviously done this before.

He was sure that Lincoln Riley would tell the Big 12 people and "I know Ruff (Ruffin McNeil) knows." I had not seen Coach that animated, and he was really perturbed at the Cyclones. "Calvin Thibodeaux (D Line Coach) will take care of them," he said. (Note: Sooners beat them 37-27 in Ames in 2018.)

The security we have at Owen Field games is the best. They really check your bag and scan you as you arrive. Everywhere we play, when we get there they are just starting up, opening the stadium, and most always, we beat the security guys into the stadium, except for OSU.

In 2017, the Bedlam game was in Stillwater. We arrived at the gate about five hours before the kickoff, and gate personnel were checking our credentials and asking our names. They have the same lady each year and seem to be harassing us. I keep the security tags we get at all the games, (Notre Dame, Ohio, and other venues) on my briefcase/bag but the OSU security lady insists on cutting them off. A real sign of strength, I suppose. We all also had preprinted Media Passes that OSU had distributed.

She asked Coach his name and was cross checking his name on some list. He kept saying "Merv Johnson." She said we do not have you down. Finally, in a very un-Coach Merv Johnson manner, he determinedly just walked on into the stadium past her, and the lady was still looking, and looking...

Coach was already in the booth sitting down as the radio crew completed the "shake down" and arrived in the press box. We each said, "You just walked past her." Coach said, "Happens every time we come up here," as he shrugged. That made me laugh.

Baker threw for 598 yards on that day in 2017 for the all-time Sooner record. I had tallied about 604 yards on my stat sheet, and I swear they changed it down to 598 because they did not want someone throwing for 600 plus yards on T Boone Field. It was another Bedlam win of 62-52. Teddy was having to get over being sad about the defense since we were just outscoring everyone. Toby tried to calm him too, but one thing was true in that we were winning every week. Sooner offense had arrived, and Baker was driving the car.

Sooner Radio Crew at the Rose Bowl 2018, Left to Right, Coach,
Teddy Lehman, Rufus Alexander, Dennis Kelly, Chris Plank, Tom
Shores, Toby Rowland, Michael Dean and Greg Blackwood.

We had a great trip to the Rose Bowl and Coach got us on the equipment and staff bus from the LA hotel. Coach said it was going to be a "tight fit." He was right. When Coach sat down by me and firmly put his hand on my shoulder and looked me square in the eye, I knew we were in for a challenge. He does not do that all the time. It was one of the legendary games in Rose Bowl history, but it was just too bad, as we lost to Georgia, in double overtime, 54-48.

Ironically it was the first ever game between Georgia and Oklahoma. They had never played but teamed up in the 1980's to challenge legally the

NCAA's hold on the television rights. The NCAA was found in violation of the Sherman Anti-Trust act, and the television rights landscape changed forever. I am still sad we lost.

I took several souvenir Rose Bowl Playoff Programs and put them in my suitcase for the trip home from California in 2018. The OU people came on the bus to the airport and announced that there was a "Hologram" in the programs that would not let our luggage go through security. I had to go to my luggage and take about five of them out. Rufus carried them for me, and we joked about having an All-American handle my stuff for me. He laughed and laughed. He always calls me Stat Kelly. Love the guy.

In 2018, Coach was moved to a "Coaches Corner" deal sitting in the booth, but not as the actual color commentator. This allowed Teddy Lehman to go to the actual color job by sitting on the front row and not being on the sideline. We added Gabe Ikard as an on-field analyst to go with Chris Plank on the sidelines.

Now Toby would set Coach up from the game situations and Coach appeared more focused since he could hear the questions. He did sound great. However, Coach did go a little long with one of his analysts at the beginning of the second half at Iowa State in Ames, and we missed the kickoff and a couple of plays. Toby is so respectful of Coach and let him go on and on.

One of the funniest things that Coach does is when Toby sets him up for a segment, or some deep football questions. Toby says, "Do you have anything to add to that Coach?" and Coach says, "Not really." I have gotten rather good at imitating the "Not really" and everyone gets a big laugh.

It sounds silly and we all laugh sometimes, but all the listeners really do want to know what he thinks. I could not tell you how many friends and acquaintances ask me what Merv thinks. And what did Merv say? Did Merv like this? Did Merv like that? The questions are many. He is one of the most knowledgeable and loved Sooner coaches ever. The thing that makes him so great is that he does not think he is great, but he is.

We started doing some "Road Trips" in around 2015-16. We drove in a sponsored Patriot Ford for a while and then a new sponsor, Landers Chevy and Dodge. We received some Love's gift cards and would stop at Love's Travel shops on the way and buy Sooner fans some snacks (and us too!) We usually do this when we ride to Iowa State and Tech, and even Baylor. In the Big XII, other than Iowa and WVU, everything is within a few hours driving. We have often left games, got in the car, and driven straight home on adrenaline and, of course, Sooner wins.

It is so fun, getting in a large Landers Chevy Tahoe, and having the Voice of the Sooners drive. Often Chris Plank will do a live radio show from the back seat while Greg Blackwood navigates. Tom Shores and I sit there talking about Sooners and sports for hours. Sometimes we get an All American to go with us, such as Rufus Alexander and it is even more fun.

Early in 2018, they decided to drop the big sideline parabolic microphone. Tom Shores was called by Eric Barnhart, VP and GM of Sooner Sports, and told that we would make him the "sideline" engineer. Tom was worried that he would lose his job, but Eric assured him he was not being eliminated. Tom is so much fun and does anything needed. Tom, Greg, and I say all the time that we cannot believe we get to do this stuff. It is a true blessing and a real "why me." How did I get so lucky? And we were paid, too.

Toby, with his quick, timely delivery may be the best in the business. He has assembled an incredible team, led by his reassuring voice and knowledge. Toby started good, and now is great! What a choice Dr. Boren and Joe made. The timing is key to his success. You never have to wait for those key things. We celebrated the 100th broadcast in 2018 as a radio crew and along with Toby, we had lots of people saying wonderful things.

Bob Stoops, with his new beard and all, came in to shake hands with everyone and say some wonderful things to Toby on his 100th game. Coach said, "He doesn't drop by all that much, it's really nice."

I do not know what I could add about the great Bob Stoops. He was all business while he was the Sooner head man. He is not one for small talk or even interactions with anyone other than players and coaches. He is a very introverted and guarded man and there are so many who think that I (and the others on the crew) just "yucked" it up with him. Bob was not "a yuck it upper" and he never was anything but all business. He would speak when I saw him, but barely. When one least expected it, he would say a "Hello." Usually this was on road trips and was when you never expected it. Sometimes it was "Is this (elevator) going up?" which always had the "up" or "down" in that stern Bob Stoops voice.

I got good at imitating him and his famous "in a great way" tone. Everyone laughs when I do it and it makes you feel good that you can say that anytime and it gets a laugh. Bob Stoops was the most comforting and consistent guy who ever ran the OU program. He was always trying to win it all and looking to get better. The Sooner fans really appreciated him, obviously.

While waiting to leave Iowa State one year, I

saw Bob Stoops talking and laughing with this nicely dressed lady just off the ramp to board the team plane (one of the few times I have flown with them). I thought, "Wow, he sure is nice and animated" and then I saw it was his wife. Oh, he was unguarded and having a fun time and we hammered I State again! That was the Bob Stoops I saw and admired.

Coach told me that Bob was nice to him and talked freely to him. I am sure it is because he has been coaching for over 50 years in some way or form. Coach said he is a lot more talkative behind closed doors in the Switzer Center.

When Merv did the broadcasts with Bob Barry, he did a "coach segment" after every game and Bob Stoops would let his "guard down" and have friendly and frank analysis after every game. Coach Merv has that effect on people, even a guy like Stoops. Sometimes it was the freest Bob would seem to the media, ever.

When Stoops retired in 2017, he also became more relaxed. It was not uncommon for Coach Stoops to fist pump you and say something on a regular basis. His suite is in the media press box area, and he is quite visible. His voice is so distinct, and it makes you really stop when you hear it coming out of a suite, and wonder, now what he is doing off the sidelines. He is really a happy man.

At the halftime of the top 10 matchup with TCU in 2017, the Sooners had a big lead. Both teams were 8-1 and vying for the Big XII championship. Walking to the restroom at halftime, the Sooners were up 38-14. I ran into Coach Stoops. He said to me, "I knew we would get it done." He was so animated and that was the most he ever said to me. He fist pumped me. It was a great half and man was he happy! We were all elated, as we were headed to a rematch in the latest Big XII championship game and the College Playoff. If Stoops thinks it is good, you know it is in a great way!

Toby added a recorded pregame segment in 2017 where Greg, Tom, and I got to reflect on the game and do a quick feature which lasted about 90 seconds. Greg would point out something he was looking for as a spotter, Tom would also reflect on something from the sidelines, and I could add a stat that was different or important to the game. It is fun and we later did get a "sponsor." Toby is always thinking and trying to do something new.

He and Ted added a neat part to the Coaches show on Tuesday. Teddy would name a game, name a time in the game, and Coach Lincoln Riley would tell the play and the result. It really shows how smart and talented Coach Riley is, along with Ted. Ted must find the play, remember it, and give enough detail that Coach can have a "chance" to remember. It is really something to watch. Coach Riley gets it about 95% of the time. If he misses, he misses by the narrowest of margins. Ted calls him a savant.

The sidelines are really hopping in 2018, and it is fun to hear all the analysis that comes from Teddy in the booth and Gabe down on the field. Plank is a true pro and gives all the listeners a real feel for aesthetics as the two players give the x's and o's. No other broadcast team has anything like it.

The Sooners played an exciting game against Army in 2018. It was action packed with scary times with the Cadets running all over the Sooners in their triple option attack. Late game heroics and a missed FG by OU at the end of regulation, had OU winning in overtime.

"That triple option still gives us fits," Coach said. No truer words were spoken. The defense never figured it out and Kenneth Murray had 28 tackles for the modern-day OU record. (Tackles were not an official stat until 2000. Apologies to Don Pfrimmer's 31 in 1967).

The Army people did something almost never seen. They virtually cleaned the Visitors' locker room after the game and left it just like it was before. Most visitors just trash the locker room and leave it in disarray, at best.

"I've never seen that happen," Coach said. "It was really something to see."

We decided after hearing that to make sure we did the same, as close as we could when we leave a "visitor's radio booth." Greg Blackwood led the way, and we try to do it each time. Of course, we rarely lose on the road, so the mood is typically good. I cannot say that for the opponents as they visit Owen Field, with over 400 losses there. That is roughly 399 times it has not been cleaned.

The ways that Teddy refers to the opponents drives them mad, I am sure. He calls K-State, KSU, TCU, Texas Christian. If he finds they do not like a reference, he uses it. He calls O-State for Oklahoma State and other names that the opponents do not like for the media to use. When you are the Butkus Award Winner and two time All American, you can do those things. His disdain for the aesthetics of the Cotton Bowl Stadium, despite his "signature moment" is a classic. He is so much fun and loved by everyone. He really tells it straight, good, or bad. Ted is a true analyst.

The Cotton Bowl has a problem. It is a venue rarely used and then is asked to be ramped up for a major event. The doors on the press box setting are hard to open and need duct tape to insure they do not lock. No one seems to ever have a key. Doors to the radio booths are unlocked on Friday, and "You better keep them propped open or they will slam shut and absolutely no one has a key."

In 2018 during the run for the Sooners when they came from behind to tie the game 45-45, late in the game the radio booth door slammed shut and locked. Greg Blackwood had a bathroom emergency and could not get the door open. The mild-mannered Greg was shouting at the usher to open the door and he was just looking through the locked door at him. It was sad and incredibly funny, afterwards. The duct tape did not last through the 48-45 loss. We never could figure out what the guy was thinking. Greg was hurting and did not see the humor, obviously.

The Texas game in 2018 was one for the ages. The Sooners got behind, and Kyler Murray spearheaded a comeback that was "almost" the greatest ever. The Sooners were behind 45-24 going into the final quarter and Kyler led them back with a 19-yard TD pass, a 67-yard TD run, and a Trey Sermon TD run with 2:38 left to tie the game at 45-45. Texas went right down the field and scored a FG with nine seconds left to defeat the Big Red 48-45. It was almost.

Coach was reflective on the trip home. "It could have been a real positive, we really have some explosive ability." And we sadly drove home with little consolation on the one that got away.

Mike Stoops was fired after the Texas game. That game was nothing different over the last few years, as the speed of the offenses, and the Sooners' speed led to many high scoring contests. I am not sure the defense and the players were ready for an offense that scored at will.

Mike was always cordial to me and was like most all the coaches. He was intent and all business. The coaches do not really know my role. They just know I am always around on game days as it takes an army of people to put out an OU game.

In the nearly seven years Mike was with the Sooners (this time), he worked from the booth upstairs. The Coach's box is on the same floor as the radio-television guys at Owen Field, and usually the same coordination on the road. It is common for the OU coach's box to be right next to ours.

The antics in the booth for Mike Stoops are legendary. He is a fiery guy, very animated, and it was not unusual to hear banging and yelling from the coach's booth. He has been on television and is the subject of several video shots. Often my friends ask if I saw him or if I know him. I usually just smile and say, "Well, sort of."

There usually is no way for us in the radio booth to see into the coaches' booth. My friend Robert Kintopp, an OU IT guy, staffs the coaches' box and does the set up and wiring. He puts paper (on the road) to cover the adjoining windows to keep folks from looking in. He has gotten to see all the ups and downs—with the ups far more than the downs. Mike had been involved in many Sooner wins, and it was sad to see him go.

Mike was replaced by Ruffin McNeal as the interim defensive coordinator. Ruffin had collaborated with Coach Riley at Tech as well as East Carolina and was one of the nicest guys. Coach Merv really liked Ruffin and said, "He has a nice style of handling players. I really do not know that these young guys were responding (to Mike) anymore." Coach Merv, however, really hated to see Mike Stoops go. He had come back to OU to be with Brent Venables again, and it never materialized. It was a sad ending to a coach who did so much.

I asked Robert how the coaches' booth was, and he said it was different, and quieter. I could agree on the road as we do not hear anything from the coaches' booth when they are neighbors.

I need to say something about Robert Kintopp (Coaches' booth) and Bryan Conkling (on field). They work on game days to make sure the telecommunications on headsets and phones between the coaches' booth and the field are flawless. They are incredibly good workers and are always fun to be around. I marvel as I often see their tireless work on cumbersome equipment, assessing it and ensuring it functions. They are essential for the coaches' communication during the game.

That 2018 TCU trip was the time coach could not get his car to turn off when we arrived at the Embassy Suites in Norman, where we regularly rendezvous. It was roaring as if its accelerator was stuck. Greg, after working anxiously for a few minutes, finally got it off. Coach said, "I guess I will have to have that looked at." It was a funny moment. Coach is always optimistic and so calm. I think most people would have been really upset.

On the trip to TCU, Coach, Greg, and I got caught in traffic in a driving rain. Coach needed to go to the bathroom, and he got so fidgety but never said a word. I noticed him leaning, talking, and talking, sort of out of character. I finally said we must stop, and we then made it to Arby's in time. Coach was so appreciative. I told him to just say something, he is so kind and hates to be a bother.

I asked Coach on the drive, who was the best lineman he ever coached, and he said Mark Hutson. He also said, "The Phillips boys were awfully good (Anthony and Jon)."

He did add that, "That big guy was the best lineman that has ever played at OU, the one who plays for the Redskins, no 71." I said, "Trent Williams" and he nodded.

"Heck," Merv said, "He (Trent) had never

played center in his life, but our center got hurt and he played one of the best games I had ever seen from a center in the Sun Bowl out in El Paso vs. Stanford. He pushed their All-American all over that field." He laughed.

"Now Keith may have the best footwork and maybe the best athlete for a big man of anyone I ever saw," Coach said. He was talking about Sooner All-American tight end, Keith Jackson. He could block, catch, and do about anything we needed done. A rousing endorsement, to put it mildly.

Merv often seems to forget names, and apologizes all the time for it, but can remember all their numbers. Pretty amazing for anyone 80 plus years old.

The Texas Tech game in 2018 was so exciting. There always seems to be wild things out in Lubbock. With the Sooners ahead only 42-40 late in the game, Tech went for two after scoring a late TD, to possibly tie the game with 6:54 left in the contest. The two point pass from Tech's Jeff Duffey was intercepted deep in the end zone and Sooner defender Robert Barnes went over 100 yards for two points for OU, to make the score 44-40 (Robert was only officially credited with a 98-yard PAT). It was one of the most incredible plays I have ever seen live. Coach said to me later, "I'll bet Reggie is sure proud," (Robert Barnes' father and former

Sooner player). It saved the day, and the Sooners won the Saturday night contest 51-46. Another shoot-out on the plains of west Texas.

Sooners went to West Virginia to have their every other year battle in the mountains. Sooners needed to win to be in the Big 12 Championship game. The Sooners gained 664 yards and WVU had 704. Kyler Murray out dueled Will Grier of WVU. He passed for over 300 yards, with three TD's and ran for 114 yards and a TD on the Friday night after Thanksgiving. The Sooners got two TDs from the defense and won the exciting game 59-56. Coach said, "He won the big trophy tonight." It was the second straight year to have a Heisman winner in Norman.

8. Miami Again And Some Great Games

We went on a charter flight to the Orange Bowl for the College Football playoff game vs. Alabama in 2018. Coach was excited to be involved in his 500th game with the Oklahoma program during the broadcast.

I asked Coach how he was and how his Christmas was, and he said it was fine but was "not looking forward to this trip, it was just a sit around and scratch your rear deal." He went on to talk about wanting to go to practice and that he could get enough information out of about 45 minutes but would be "trapped there for about 4-5 hours".

We got to sit in the lobby of the Diplomat Hilton on Hollywood Beach, FL and talk on one of the off days. Lance Barrow, coordinating producer of golf for CBS Sports, came by and chatted with us. His daughter was an OU alum and Lance is a fellow Church of Christ guy. We talked about our common mission experiences, acapella versus live music, and being on the border of Mexico and around Piedras Negras. He is the coordinating producer and has won Emmys for the CBS NFL coverage, The Master's Golf, etc. He is kind of a big deal but is very cordial and is a golf television legend.

Lance could really tell interesting, candid, and funny stuff. He said that Frank Chirkinian, the legendary inventor of golf on TV gave an answer to a question once that was astounding. He (Frank) was asked why CBS did such a fantastic job and were the best at doing golf on TV. Lance said anxiously, "Chirkinian said because we know when to go to commercials." This sounded easy and simple but was true. "It is all in the timing," Lance said. "So many holes, shots, and they never miss a real live moment." What a profound comment.

Chikinian was Lance's boss and mentor at CBS. He also told us of his work with Pat Summerall, Ken Venturi, and Tom Brookshire. A true broadcast legend. I loved every minute of talking with him.

Coach sat there and did not say a word as Lance told his tales with so many interesting and funny things. Coach had this serene look as he told his stories. After he left, Coach said to me, "He sure was nice, and has lots of information." I really thought that was funny.

I ran into Toby Keith on the elevator of the Diplomat. He said the SEC is "so overrated" and other choice words. He talked freely to me and told me we were doing a fantastic job on the radio. Heck, you do not get that stuff as a lowly CPA. The Sooners are magic.

The halftimes at the Orange Bowl are legendary. This year (2018) they had Hip Hop Artist, Flo Rida. It was so loud and there was smoke. I asked Coach if he liked it and he said, "It's ok, I guess, but you can't see it or even hear it." He was right. I never could even see the guy. It did get rave reviews, guess I am a poor critic.

Coach again added his wisdom on the post-game to Sooner Nation as the Sooners lost the Orange Bowl to Alabama and it was his 500th game. "Do not go out and get a razor now. There were about 130 teams in college football who were not here. We can always take something from that." He always adds the reality of life to it. He said later to me "This is the first time I have ever been a loser to Alabama. I beat them at Notre Dame too, and OU." The frantic comeback by the Sooners, led by Kyler Murray, was not enough.

Kyler Murray finished the 2018 season with over 4,000 yards passing and 1,000 rushing, only second guy to ever do that in the history of the college game.

There were several recorded accolades for Coach during the Orange bowl. Toby Keith, Switzer, Joe Washington to name just a few. When he was asked about the 500th, he said, "He didn't think he would make 1,000." Everyone laughed. He was reflective after the Orange Bowl game. He said, "This was my life and I sure liked hanging with you guys, even though I didn't add much." We all (to a man) told him how much we wanted him there with us.

After the game with our gallant comeback attempt had ended, and we were winding down the show (a 45-34 loss), I told him in the postgame that the Alabama radio crew had already gone home. He laughed and said, "We are on after a game more than anyone I have seen. I can see it after a home game as people travel home in their cars, but not so much in the road games. They have other things to do and heck it is 1 am. We interview all these players and we do so much talk that they do not have any opportunity to talk." There were smiles all around.

We later waited as Michael Dean closed for the year and removed all the wires from the equipment. He has a tradition which would not let us do much, so we (all but Gabe who hit the road to parts unknown) sat around.

Coach reflected on how the "guy from Notre Dame (Brian Kelly) is always Coach of the Year. He is again for the second time; I cannot really understand." Someone said it is the "they are from Notre Dame deal." I joked at coach, "How is that at Notre Dame, Coach? Did you like that when you were there?" He chuckled back at me.

We flew back early the next day (Sunday the 30th) after the Orange Bowl on a chartered flight. As we separated upon arrival in OKC, many got on the bus to head back to Norman and the few others left from AAR terminal at Will Rogers Airport. Coach would be on the bus to Norman, and I had left my car at Will Rogers Airport in OKC. It was windy and cold and was a sharp contrast from the 80 plus degrees and humidity of Miami.

I told him good-bye as we parted in the frigid wind. I told him I would be calling him, and I loved him. He said he loved me too. I always treasure my time with him. I am getting an opportunity to be with one of the finest people I have known.

The spring game came in 2019 and the Sooners had the most exciting transfer since Joe Don Looney. Jalen Hurts, of Alabama QB fame, enrolled as a graduate transfer. The game was rescheduled to Friday night on short notice due to possible rain and even a possibility of snow.

The game was extraordinarily successful and

had an attendance of around 50,000 at the cool 7:30 pm Friday affair. Coach Merv was honored by Joe C for his 500th game with the Sooners. Merv often commented how great Joe was to him and was a real inspiration.

Coach had told us he needed to run down to the field. The spring game is a festive event with all sorts of alumni events, speakers, etc., so it was no big deal. We all looked down on the field and there was Coach on the big scoreboard video screen accepting an award with the crowd roaring. What a guy, never said a word. Just came back and sat down. We all just laughed since it was vintage Coach.

The Company (Learfield) saw a need to change the producer/engineering situation in 2019 and we added Drake Diacon to the group. Drake is a young radio guy with a University of Oklahoma degree and a rising star in the technology, the radio business, and knew radio-scanning stuff. He was hired to shadow Michael Dean who has over 30 years with the group. Michael was planning to work for two more years as Drake learned from Michael and they would take the reins for Sooner broadcasts. I do not know what was going on, as I have only been in the broadcasting business for about 40 years. It seemed like a way to gracefully move into a more modern setting and let Michael retire.

In 2019, there apparently was a need to change

the travel arrangements for the crew. Learfield merged with IMG, the two biggest college sports broadcasters radio groups became "Learfield-IMG College." Now that big mouthful saw there should be a reduction of radio personnel to travel with OU, especially on team flights. Our crew was the largest in the company. Tom Shores and Rufus Alexander were removed from the travel squad and were only at home and the Texas games. There are ten to eleven on the crew and somehow, we keep growing. It appeared, based on the number of credentials we get from other teams, we seemed to irritate someone, somewhere, I guess. (It is hard to imagine that Kansas, Tech, and Iowa State care about credentials. They are glad anyone comes at all usually.)

We hated to see that, especially for Tom. He lived for the Sooners and in years gone by would drive or personally pay to fly to the games and meet the broadcast crew in places like Seattle, Oregon, LA, etc. We all missed Rufus too. A more fun guy cannot be found.

Coach sat down with me and wrote out the seasons (while sitting in the un-airconditioned press box at Iowa St.) he had been doing football. It was 69 that he scribbled out. And he said he has been involved with only three teams (his high school team, Arkansas in 1964, and Oklahoma in 2000) that were undefeated. He also has only been associated with four teams that lost more than they won. (One at Arkansas, and three at OU.) He was proud of that, it is about 6%. That is incredible.

He wanted the OU job when Switzer left in 1989, but there was a regent from Tulsa that wanted Gary Gibbs, so he got the job. "I liked him, (Gibbs)" Merv quipped, "He was a good coach, but he did not like the special things that a head coach had to do, he liked to study film, and game plan." Gibbs got the head job, but Coach Merv is now the popular legend. Life is interesting.

He told me again that he was there the last time Iowa State won over OU in Ames in 1960. He said he was scouting "live" for that game in 1960. Coach said there was a play that OU ran that he could not really catch the formation and the blocking (with the naked eye). Coach scribbled out a T formation on the sheet. He said OU scored twice on Mizzou using that play the next week. He chuckled. I will keep that sheet forever.

Coach was in Norman in 1960 when Missouri defeated OU 41-19 (12 of the 19 points were using the play), one of Mizzou's biggest wins and Bud's worst defeats. It was one week removed from the Iowa State loss and was at that time only the fourth loss ever in conference play by a Bud team. Mizzou was ranked Number 2 and the Sooners were on the way to Bud's only losing season. Merv's scouting was good.

The teams exchanged films for scouting purposes sometimes, and it was Coach's job, after scouting OU, to exchange the films with the OU coaches. Coach went to the Sooner locker room after the Mizzou win and knocked on the door and it quickly opened, "and there was Bud Wilkinson." Coach said I stumbled and mumbled my way to getting the films exchanged.

"He did not lose very often, but was really nice to me," Coach said. Coach had never met or interacted with him until that day.

I was able to ride by myself with Coach to the OU/TX game in 2018. He got reflective about Notre Dame and beating Texas in 1977.

Coach said, "Lost one of the first games of the year (1977) to Ole Miss (was second game) about 20-13 or so, and it was about 110 degrees. We had a real problem getting Devine to go with our QB (Montana). Got him straightened out though. Devine wanted to go with a younger guy, and it cost us down in Mississippi, but we got him straight. And we never lost again. Started the year 1-1 or so, did not lose again."

"Joe was a no-nonsense guy and didn't go for some of the stuff," he said.

"He was easy to coach, he forgot each play and

moved on. Devine thought he was not serious enough, he did not seem to worry enough, I guess. He was as good as I ever saw at not worrying about what happened and went on to the next play."

I asked Coach about the big comeback that Irish had against Houston in the 1979 Cotton Bowl (from 23 points down) at the end of the 1978 season. He said that Joe had hypothermia and they had to keep him from "freezing up." It is often referred to as the "Chicken Soup Game," as they fed him Chicken bouillon on the sidelines due to a below zero wind chill.

Joe Montana threw a touchdown pass to win the game as time expired. I asked coach what play he called. Coach said, "I just looked at him, threw up my hands and said whatever you want." He hit a guy in the corner end zone line to cap a great college career. It has been considered by many as one of the most important bowl games ever, and it was Coach's final game as a member of the Notre Dame staff.

Coach said, "We had about six guys that got thrown off the Notre Dame team in 1974 under Ara Parseghian. Devine worked to get them back on the team. They were good kids but had broken some rules in the dorm. They were valuable players and helped Notre Dame win a National Championship and a bunch of games." Ross Browner, Al

Hunter, and Willie Fry to name a few, all great and incredibly talented players.

I asked Coach if he liked being on the field or in the booth. He said he did not mind either, but really liked looking right at the players and getting to interact with them. I asked him who was his counterpart in the booth at Notre Dame and he said, "Oh I know his name, boy was he a real talker. I would take the headset off and hang it on my belt until we gave up the ball or scored and he would still be talking."

I also inquired if he ever played or coached against Bear Bryant. He said they played against him at Notre Dame (beat them in 1975 and 1976), and he played against him when he was a senior at Mizzou and Bear was at A&M.

He said Coach Broyles (in his only year in Mizzou) told him a while after that game in Columbia, that Bear said to him in pregame "you don't have very many players." I asked coach if they won, and he said, "Shoot no. Lost 28-0." I am sure Coach Broyles leaving for Arkansas after one year at Mizzou was aided by the "not very many players."

Coach Merv looking over the field as the Sooners
win another one. In his analyst seat.

Coach remarked that he was sure sad to see Tom Shores removed from the traveling group. "He sure enjoyed traveling with us," Coach said to me as we walked the concourse around the legendary Rose Bowl stadium. "Heck, I did not find out I was coming until yesterday about 4pm," Coach said.

The out-of-town travel is always an adventure with the Sooners. It is common to find out on Tuesday or Wednesday of the game week whether we are on the travel list for the "team plane" or a separate staff plane or driving. It is bizarre that they do not know who is going. Surely, I just do not get the problems they have routing and collaborating with alumni, staff, special requests, and such. It is a nightmare, I am sure. Most every year we only have one or two games where we travel on a plane. Those games are usually West Virginia, Iowa State, and a non-conference foe like Tennessee, Ohio State, UCLA, et al. The SEC will be an interesting new challenge. All I know is it will be first class.

We often do not know where we are staying. I could not tell you the number of friends who asked me where we were staying, when we were going. I just have to say, "I have no idea." More often they just look at me and most say "Really?" Sounds silly, but it is true. It is usually the team hotel, but we change them quite often. The accommodations are always first-rate and the Sooner players and staff take virtually the whole hotel.

It is impressive to have the freeways of Los Angeles stopped by groups of CHIPS and LA Police as we maneuvered through the Friday afternoon traffic the 20 miles or so from LAX to Glendale, CA for the team hotel, the Glendale Hilton. It is spectacular and that is putting it mildly.

We had dinner with the whole radio crew a few blocks from the hotel in Glendale. We all walked a few blocks to a Mexican restaurant and were able to hear some stories from Coach. He told us about Wendell Mosley, the coach with him on Switzer's staff. Coach said Wendell "went on a recruiting trip, because he was a good one, on a Friday and later presented his expense report" (to Barry Switzer on his return). Barry said, "What happened, Wendell, did you jack up your car and run it full throttle all weekend to get that many miles?" Coach said Wendell could really recruit, but even he could not drive that many miles. There were smiles all around.

On returning to the hotel, Coach led the way. Toby said, "What does that say about us when an 80-year-old man is leading us?" Sure enough, as we walked thru the dark, he led us right back to the Hilton (on a different route than our original jaunt).

The Sooners went on to the Rose Bowl stadium (for the 5th total time) and shellacked UCLA 48-14. It was not much of a game, but you cannot beat the setting. Last time the Sooners won in California (regular season) was 1990 (UCLA 34-14). Everyone was so optimistic. (Sooners won 2003 Rose and 2005 Holiday Bowls.)

After the UCLA game, we broke down the equipment to get on the team plane. I was unofficially assigned the duty to take Coach to the bus and make sure they waited for all of the crew as the radio equipment was packed for home.

We wandered off towards the south entrance near the place where we had been dropped off earlier on the charter bus. Coach had a little trouble seeing, and wanted to get on the UCLA pep bus, but I convinced him it was the wrong one. He said he was sure glad I was with him. He reiterated to me again, that "he was not helping much, and should just quit after this year." I told him to keep on doing it as long as he wants, everyone wants him, and he helps add so much levity to the crazy football world.

Coach said as we drove through the streets of LA that our Center, Creed Humphry (Number 56) was the best lineman we had ever had at Oklahoma.

"71 (Trent Williams) was awfully good, but this kid locks in, and he keeps driving on and on. He may be the best." I will think about that one. A kid from Shawnee, OK high may be the best Sooner to ever play on the offensive line.

Sooners went on to go 5-0 early in the season after a win at Kansas. Coach was reflecting on the Missouri team that lost to KU in 1960. He said it was the only time ever they (Mizzou) had a chance to be undefeated, but KU used an ineligible player.

"That guy was good (Bert Coan), and we lost at Columbia 23 to 7. It may be their only time they will have a chance to win a National Championship." There was a true melancholy in his voice. Of all the teams we play, Coach really does not have any fondness for Kansas. That is about par for a former Mizzou player.

I talked to him about Coach Devine and then Broyles. Coach said, "Devine left me alone. I liked working for him, but Broyles was a little better coach. Broyles could really get good teams and we always seemed to be playing Texas. Broyles could play golf all day long with him (Darrell Royal) and they would just skip around the golf course. Might play 54 holes or more in a day."

Coach then said, "Next week will be the 58th time to look across the field against Texas." He had been facing Texas for about as long as I was alive, I told him. That was most of my life. He then said that Broyles really was a good judge of people. He had a "real knack for knowing if a guy could help and lead players." His record of hiring Switzer, Merv, Johnny Majors, Jim Mackenzie, and Jimmy Johnson, to name a few, was legendary. He also said Pat Jones was a guy who really excelled. He was also reflective about the Arkansas program. "They should have joined the Big 12, they have never won a conference championship in the SEC, and when they left the conference they were in, that cut off all their ties to Texas. It is impossible for them when they do not get many Texas high school players."

Greg Blackwood came in during the West Virginia game with a new hat. It said "405" on it and he got it to razz Chris Plank. Chris is a "918" area code guy and we always laugh when he refers to Tulsa and eastern Oklahoma guys as "918" guys. It was funny.

During the Kansas game, Drake and Michael got Coach a headset that muffled the crowd noise, and he could only hear Toby and Teddy in his ear. He was so confident and made some great comments, maybe the best of the year.

He made a comment about Kansas' Pooka Williams, the talented running back that gained over 200 yards against the Sooners in 2018 and ran wild during the first half. He was held to 137 yards in 2019 for the day.

"That Pookie is good, and you have to hold on to get him. He's good." It was so funny calling him "Pookie," but it was a compliment of the highest regard for the guy.

I broke my shoulder while visiting a sick man from our church at the OU Medical center in early season 2019. No real reason for my accident, just an old guy falling. I knew it when it happened, and it was the same left arm I broke in the Junior High "Oklahoma drill." I was at the mercy of others to drive to the games and had the privilege of riding with Toby to Kansas and K State. He is such a good guy, and really likes to "roll with Rowland" in his big Chevrolet.

Coach Merv drove to Fayetteville, AR alone on Friday before the WVU game and drove straight back. He went to a 50-year celebration of the 1969 team, and it is No 1 vs No 2 battle between Arkansas and Texas, that Texas won 15-14. He said he saw about 70 people that were somehow a part of that team.

"I was lucky they all had name tags around their necks," he laughed. "I would not know some of them, though I coached and recruited them."

"I got caught in a rainstorm and got turned around getting back on I-35. I was going the wrong way." I told him I would be glad to drive him, but I think he would rather not bother me and wants to do it himself. He got back to Norman at 3 am and we had an 11 am kick off. What a trooper.

Tom Shores drove Coach and me to the 2019 Texas game. We drove with his grandson Jack, as well. It was fun. Coach was having a fun time, and we enjoyed being with him.

We stopped at the truck stop or car stop, Bucees, for gas just outside of Denton. It is known as the porcelain palace with so many gas pumps and more. It was so funny to see Coach's amazement as he walked among the masses who were shopping for grills, clothes, jerky, and all types of fresh food and drinks. It was amazing how many people recognized him and said so many wonderful things.

He was so gracious and smiled and greeted them all. When we got back into Tom's car after being inside Buc-ees, he said that was "quite a marvelous place." It is impressive.

The 2019 Sooners took care of Texas 34-27, and we rolled out of town undefeated. Coach said it is so big to beat them. He also said, "We sure spend a lot of time talking about it, though." Jack got to see his first ever OU/Texas game, and Coach took him around the locker room and the stadium. He was excited.

Coach could always produce some Fletcher's corn dogs if the Sooners win. I never knew how he did it, he would just slip away and come into the radio booth a few minutes after the end of the game with about six corn dogs. I asked him how he got them, and he just winked.

We traveled to Manhattan, KS and the Sooners played the Wildcats on the last Saturday of October. I visited Coach Merv about the development of Kansas State. He laughed about seeing the KSU players work out while they played in Norman in 1980. "They were really small and didn't look like college players." We talked about the 1981 game where the Sooners won 28-21 and Darrell Shepherd had a great game. What a thrill to sit with Coach on road games as we wait for the start of the games. He is open and kind to sit and relive these things.

"We were down about 21-6 at halftime of that game," Coach quipped. "They had multiple on-side kicks." We talked about that game and how tough it was in 1981 while waiting before the kick-off in 2019. Little did we know.

The 1981 game was a big come from behind victory for the Sooners, after K State took a stunning 21-6 halftime lead. Linebacker Jackie Shipp was quoted as saying, "We did not expect them to move the ball that well on us. We played lackadaisical in the first half, and we had to fight for our life." The Cats used extremely rare multiple on-side kicks where the kicker recovered their own on-side kicks and the Sooners had only two possessions in the first half and at one time was down in time of possession by 21:41 to OU's 1:46. The Sooners ran 15 plays in the first half to KSU's 49.

I never dreamed that an onside kick and the controversy that surrounded it would be the deciding factor as the Wildcats would upset the 2019 Sooners, coming in at 7-0 and 5th ranked by 48-41.

Sooners only had six plays in the 3rd quarter and were outscored 24-0, before the big comeback started. Sooners were down 48-23. OU ran off 18 unanswered points and on-side kicked the ball that ricocheted off our blocked player (Trejan Bridges) and was recovered by OU on the Cat 37. This play was reviewed and somehow was given to KSU with

1:42 left. It was all over and the Big 12 and multiple referee analogics were cited. Sooners had given up eight straight scoring drives vs the Cats, before the 18-point desperate onslaught.

Sooners were back on the outside of the play-offs. Sooners also gave up six rushing touchdowns for only the fourth time ever. The three others were to Colorado (1968 and 1994) and Nebraska in 1997. However, we had no chance to win or even tie any of those games.

"Never thought it was their ball on the on-side kick," Coach said. And he became the post-game counselor again telling folks to not "get out the razors." K State had done an impossible task.

The Sooners travelled to Baylor in 2019 and took on an undefeated Baylor team that was 9-0. The game was on a Saturday night and mirrored the same type of game as the one in 2015. At that time, Baylor had won 20 in a row and were rated fourth in the country and the Sooners were 12th. This particular year, Sooners were 10th ranked in the country and Baylor was 13th.

The game had a weird feel. The Baylor crowd screamed "OU sucks" during the national anthem and the anthem was played in an off key. Then a "Baptist Pastor" who was announced as a Baylor Alum gave an invocation with reference to Baylor winning and finished the prayer with "Sic 'em

Jesus." It stunned the obvious partisan crowd followed by a brief loud rumble and the game was on.

Sooners had a disastrous first half and fell behind 28-3 and finally 31-10 at halftime. Coach was distraught and was seen with his head in his hands all bent over. I had not seen him like that before.

The place was rocking, and this may have been the loudest crowd ever (other than the Cotton Bowl). The Baylor people in the hallway outside our radio booth were really laughing and singing, and we were asking "How did you like the first half?" It seemed the Bear faithful did not want Art Briles back but wanted his killer attitude. I had not seen that in Waco since he left and all the scandal. However, then came the second half.

Sooners ran 58 plays to Baylor's 16 in the second half and held Baylor scoreless. The Sooners scored 24 unanswered points and had the **biggest comeback in the long history of OU football**. Coach said, "This is one I will never forget." He was really stunned, as were everyone there, especially the Baylor faithful. Jalen Hurts went from a disaster to a Heisman finalist. Sooners won 34-31 and the Big XII race was on.

The Dallas Morning News reportedly said, "Pastor called on Sic 'em Jesus and he was busy." Many hung heads in green and gold. Coach also said, "There were a lot of penalties in the first half that were not called." He never complains about the refs. Interesting observation.

The Baylor game had so many memorable plays for the Sooners, right at 40 instances once they got behind, almost all from the second half. I later outlined all forty and sent them to all the radio crew in a word document. It was amazing.

There was no one around the press box when we completed the post-game show at BU. All the yelling was over for the Bears. Virtually no one around from the press box to the car (that is common on the road due to the Sooner successes). It was one of the greatest drives home ever!! **What A ball game**!

Coach said, "That was quite a list you put together with all those plays. That was really something to see." It was a game for the ages. Everyone felt the season had been saved for the OU football team and fans.

Sooners played the TCU Horned Frogs in the last home game of 2019, and Coach came into the booth with a big blue bandage on. He had had a wreck and was blindsided by another vehicle at a Norman intersection. Coach had been pried from his car, which was totaled. He also cut his left hand. We are so glad it was not worse. Merv was injured on Friday and went back to work on Saturday night. What a trooper.

The team went back to Arlington and another Big 12 Championship in early December 2019. The Sooners had to play Baylor for the second time after the come-back win at Baylor earlier in November. Last year at this time, the Sooners averaged 264 yards rushing a game, and this year 260 yards a game. In 2018, they averaged 320 yards passing and 2019, 304. All this is comparable, just like identical 11-1 records, but the real change was the opponents have 98 fewer points scored this year and almost 1,400 fewer yards gained. The one thing that has for sure **not** changed, the Sooners won another Big 12 championship, their fifth in a row (three in a row in the rematch games between the first and second seeded teams).

The Sooner defense was formidable and played to a 30-23 OT win. Tom Shores got to go to the game (apparently championships do not count on the road ban), and he drove us down with Coach to Texas. Riding along I asked Coach about Jerry Jones. He said, "Jerry was always successful, even as a young player at multiple positions. He really has really done well."

Coach said to me on the way home, "Cee Dee was really something, he just kept running and running, that was one to remember." He was the player of the game and had a 71-yard catch and run in the first quarter.

The Sooners had to endure a heroic Baylor effort using a true freshman quarterback who had (up until the Champ game) only three snaps in 2019. Jacob Zeno had two throws for 159 yards which accounted for 60% of their output and almost spoiled OU. Tre Brown saved the day by running down a sure touchdown pass to a Baylor receiver (and Olympic type runner and All-American sprinter) Chris Platt to force a FG and set up the OT final. Brown had saved the day in 2018, sacking the Texas QB in the end zone and ending Texas chances. The Sooners had won their 52nd straight game when leading at the end of the third quarter. Their last loss had been in 2014 (OSU re-punt game) in overtime, 38-35.

Tre Brown's run down of Platt was one of the greatest plays (not unlike his safety against Texas) I had seen with my own eyes. Ironically, both plays for Tre (one in 2018 and one in 2019) happened near the same spot on the same field.

Coach agreed with me and just shook his head when we reviewed it on the drive home. He was so relieved. He still lived and died like a coach, even in his eighties. He was struggling to hear, however.

Merv Johnson had just seen/coached/called his 513th Sooner game. He said to me, "I really have not missed a game since 1958. That is two (years) at Arkansas, two at Missouri, thirteen at Arkansas, four at Notre Dame and now every game since

1979 at Oklahoma. Shoot, I do not think I have ever missed one, even as a player."

I mentioned to him that it must have been hard to leave Arkansas after 13 seasons, which is a long time to coach in one spot. Coach said, "It was a different place, and was a different area (Notre Dame). They had so much snow, and you had to drive 90 miles or so to Chicago to fly and recruit and get anywhere. It is cold there." He said it was a place where all the recruits knew about you and were really welcoming. Arkansas was a "little harder sell, and Notre Dame was a lot like Oklahoma in recruiting players."

We left Coach after the drive home at his new "Toyota Off-Road" Pickup he bought after his wreck. He had parked his truck at the Embassy Suites parking lot in Norman and Tom Shores drove us to Arlington and Jerry World. He said, "Thanks so much for putting up with me. I cannot remember things anymore and cannot hear, and that is a bad combination." We all laughed and assured him we really wanted to be with him, and he was loved. We reiterated we really needed him and wanted him to continue.

We told him we would see him in three weeks as we were almost sure (and it happened) we would be off to the College Football Playoffs for the third straight year. "Oh, I will see you sooner than that (how prophetic)," he said. I was not sure what he meant but smiled and felt all warm inside. Just like always.

9. End Of An Era

On Sunday before the 2019 playoff game, Toby texted all of us on the radio crew saying Coach was in a serious car accident and was "med flighted to OU Medical. Hopefully, a good prognosis was coming soon, and he was with his family."

I left home at once for downtown and the OU Medical Center. I am always apprehensive about going to OU Medical, where I fell earlier that fall. I always make a point of going to another door, even if I park far away.

Switzer was there, Joe C, Doc Schnebel, Toby, and of course all of Coach's family. He had been driving back from seeing family in Missouri and ran into a parked car near the Perry, OK exit, on I-35.

Thank goodness he did not hit anyone, but he had multiple contusions, a tearing of his face, skin, and broken ribs. He was reportedly giving the nurses a tough time and was sure sorry he was getting "fussed over." This is typical of Coach. The group of people who were in the waiting room began to sigh a real sigh of relief. The family was so gracious as their prayers were answered. Brock Schnebel, MD, and team physician gave a positive report. Toby asked him on the side if "we could keep the streak alive," we got 513 in a row and we need him in ATL. We all knew that was a real stretch. We were so relieved that he had not lost his life. He had hit an abandoned vehicle on I-35 north near Perry, OK.

While waiting, Joe C began telling Toby and me about the Missouri debacle when Merv was in an interview there in late 1984. Woody Widenhoffer got the job and Joe was, as he said, "lowly Assistant AD" at Mizzou at the time. Joe said it was such a debacle of a process and was the first time he had met Merv. So many of the Mizzou people knew and fondly talked about Merv and many called him Mervin.

Joe said he ran into John Cooper (former Tulsa and Ohio State Coach) at the Ohio State game in 2017, who along with Merv were the frontrunners (at one time) for the Mizzou job. Joe said they discussed that hiring fiasco and, "Cooper said it was the worst process ever and somehow the Chancellor of Mizzou got involved and Woody was awarded the job at the last minute."

Coach Switzer came by as the group was leaving after hearing the good report from the Doctor, and Joe said to Switzer, "Remember the Woody interview when Merv was a candidate?"

Switzer said, "Oh yeah, Woody brought in all these pro assistants, and they did not know what they were doing, especially when they played us. I was in a coaches' association meeting in Houston in about '88 and RC Slocum, Jackie Sherrell, Pat Jones, and I were sitting around, and Woody came by and said, 'Switzer, I am going to kick your rear.'" I said, "Woody, we hung 77 on you this year (1987). How is that going to happen?" We all roared laughing.

I visited with Coach's son-in-law Michael and told him that all of us radio guys have been trying to keep him from driving. We both agreed and are convinced that his driving days were over. I told him I had volunteered to take him to Fayetteville and other places, and I knew his grandsons would as well. The saga of an aged parent driving is one of the great challenges of adulthood. The powdered butt syndrome was in action.

We all assured the Johnson family about the prayers, love, and concern and we would check on Coach again tomorrow as the entourage of people left the family waiting area.

I went out to visit with Coach in his hospital

room at OU Medical center in Oklahoma City, on the way to the airport, on December 26th. The charter flight to the Peach Bowl playoff game was leaving from Will Rogers Airport later that day.

He was sitting up, with about 100 staples in his head and talking about going. He said he could go if he had more days to recuperate. He told one of the nurses that "he sure hoped he wasn't keeping them from someone who needed it, by coming and helping him." It was vintage Coach. It was sure funny, seeing all those bandages and his face all black and blue, sitting there all dressed in his new Air Jordan shoes.

Talked with his son Jeff, and he said he spent about an hour or so looking for his clothes. He really thought he may just "check out and head home." We all smiled.

Tyler Palmateer of the Norman Transcript and Berry Tramel of the Oklahoman wrote about Coach during our stay in Atlanta. They both authored nice articles about the 513-game streak and how much we all missed Coach.

From the first game with Iowa on September 15, 1979, with the Sooners beating a Bobby Stoops Hawkeye team 21-6, to the OU Baylor rematch (winning 30-23) in the Big XII Championship game, December 7, 2019, in Arlington it had been quite a ride. 33 Bowl games. Two National Championships (2000, 1985). Started and ended with wins.

Toby had wonderful things to say to multiple news outlets as did the others in the radio group. They all told of the real sadness of missing him, to elation about saving him from almost sure death. A real wave of emotions in the wake of the biggest game of the year.

We hung Coach's credential up in the Booth and it was different not having him sitting there. I missed his giving me his patented grin (no matter the score) and his calming and direct comments, which were usually always on point.

We found out right about game time that Coach had been discharged from OU Medical and now was in Norman at a Rehab facility where he could rest and get care. He was still a little confused but making progress, according to his son Jeff. We were all glad.

In a way, I am happy Coach could only see the LSU game from afar. We were never in the game and were routed 63-28. It was the worst game I had seen since the 2004 Orange Bowl hammering USC gave the Sooners. Only problem, I had to stay at this one to the end. It was a sad ending for Jalen Hurts and Cee Dee Lamb and overshadowed the fifth straight Big 12 Championship and 12-win season with wins over Texas and OSU. All their successes were forgotten in a mess of a game. At least Coach did not have to endure the flight home.

I had said to Toby over the headset during a time out early in the game, "This game sure felt like the first time I took the CPA exam. I got about twenty minutes into the test and knew I did not prepare correctly and needed significantly more study time, but still had three days left to go to complete the test." We had a sad chuckle as Toby and all the guys knew exactly what I meant.

Joe Burrow, the new Heisman Trophy winner for LSU, routed the Sooners with seven touchdown passes in the first half. I looked up in the Game Notes the "Last time" section under six TD passes by an opponent (it did not even go to seven) and it said, "Under research." I knew the Sooners were in big trouble. We could not get out of there fast enough and get back to Oklahoma.

The Sooners had produced a Heisman runner up (Hurts), a consensus All-American in Cee Dee Lamb, and had a kicker Gabe Brkic who did not miss a field goal or extra point all year. No one had scored that many points as a kicker in a year with NO misses. No one.

Coach spent a week or so at the Jim Thorpe Rehabilitation Center in South OKC. He was very mobile when I visited him. He had the biggest scar on his forehead. He told me he was "Glad I didn't have to see the loss to LSU." Coach showed me several times the picture of him and all his seven grandkids, he is so proud of them...Haley, Riley, Charlie, Davis, Press, Macy, and Jack.

He wanted to talk about the Dallas Cowboys and their new coach, Mike McCarthy (who was the former Packer head man). He talked several minutes about Jerry Jones and his hirings. Coach then told me he had "talked to Jerry (Jones)" in the late 90's about being an assistant with the Dallas Cowboys. He said that Jerry did not have a fit for him at that time, so Coach told him to forget about it. He really did not want anyone to know they were talking. That would have been something. He would go from the worst deal ever (John Blake's regime) to America's team.

Coach was proud of Jerry and all he had done and was sure he wanted him to come down to Dallas in some capacity, but Merv nixed it. He told me again about how they moved his (Jerry's) position around and "even made a fullback out of him once" and he was on that great undefeated 1964 Arkansas team. He soon left the rehab center to stay with his daughter Jan, who lives near him.

I called him on his cell phone a week or so later. I really did not know if he had his phone back since it was in the wreck. He sounded good and wanted to know how I was doing. This is very typical of him. It is always about you and not him. Coach said, "I've been raking leaves with a big scar is all." I laughed aloud. The pictures of his truck after the wreck were so incredibly frightening, he was lucky to be alive.

Coach had breakfast with Coach Switzer, Jerry Pettibone, and other former Sooner coaches and players a few weeks later, and it was posted on social media. It was so great to see him out. Toby's reaction on Twitter was "Merv!!!" What a proper response. It was great to see him.

Visited via phone with him later that week in February and he said he was "sleeping over at his daughters but was going up four or five times a day to his house to feed the old cat and all." He sounded good, and it was great to hear his calming voice. He said the lunch with Switzer was nice and a real "surprise."

There are few people in a lifetime that make you feel good just by hearing their voice. Coach Merv is one of those for me. You always feel warm inside when he speaks.

The pandemic in 2020 hampered all my interactions with Merv, and many others. There was no spring ball or much else. From March 13 on, there was not much.

I did call Coach's son Jeff and told him I had been writing the stuff that had happened, especially since I had been working and traveling with him. I sent him what I had compiled, and he gave me a story that summed coach up.

The Following Is Per Jeff Johnson:

One story he most likely will not remember, but it is so vivid, like it happened yesterday—I feel I must share (as I will mention this at his funeral the day he goes to be with Christ in heaven):

- In 1995, OU was playing OSU in Norman—the last game coached by Schellenberger. OU lost to a bad OSU team 12-0. Merv was very uneasy that season, as he was always looking over his shoulder because he was not one of Howard's guys. He oversaw special teams by title only, yet he never worked with any unit because the other coaches were assigned those duties. The special teams were horrendous—I bet if you looked, they set a record that season for most punts getting blocked—it seemed like one a game. After the game, I walked into the locker room, and he was giving a radio interview with Eschbach or someone. They were asking him about blocked punts, etc., and the horrific play of the special teams. He stated that his shoulders were "broad and his back was strong," and he would face the criticism head on.

- He leaves the interview, gives me a hug, I am 27 and married with no kids at the time, and we walk back to get his belongings. He tells me he loves me, and that he had no idea what was going to happen to him with Howard — most likely be fired. As we walked out of the locker room (about 60-90 minutes after the game) to his car, the OSU fans were celebrating wildly.

- Standing at the gate there was a family — a husband, wife, and a son who was in his late teens or early 20's, severely handicapped in a wheelchair. There was no one within 200 yards of us. The place was empty. As we walked through the gate to the lot, they stopped Merv and asked for his autograph in the program. They were from Western Oklahoma, told him they had waited specifically for him, as he was their favorite coach and they had followed him for years. First, he shook hands and told them he was sorry about the way OU played and the loss. He signed the program, and then took a picture with the young man. He visited about the QB play briefly, and that he hoped next year would be better. This lasted about five minutes, and both groups thanked each other and walked away.

• As we were walking to the car, he stopped me, put his arm around me, looked me in the eye and stated, "There are so many more important things in life other than football. Do not you ever forget that. Now, let's get something to eat." Jeff Johnson

I called Coach in July of 2020 to check and see how he was doing. The call went to voice mail, and he called me back a couple of days later. He sounded good and he said he was mowing yards, watering, and trying to stay cool. He asked me how I was doing as always. I later got a call from him which I often do, and he said he just dialed me by mistake.

No matter what I am doing, he calls when I am concerned or sad about something. Hearing that distinctive voice always lifts my spirits.

I received another call on Saturday, August 15, 2020. It was from Coach and honestly, I thought it was one of those mistake calls. He asked me how I was doing, and he said that he had just read what I had written and it "brought tears to my eyes." He had found a copy that I had sent to Jeff and was in "some book" there at his house. He said so many flattering things about what I had written and said several times that "I must have talked to so many people."

I reiterated to Coach, that all of it was what I had seen and was what we had visited while we waited for kick offs, especially while on the road. He laughed and was the same old coach.

I later called Coach's daughter and told her I wanted to see Coach. She was gracious and said he would love it. I went down to his house on August 25, 2020, and spent time with him. He was happy and showed me his awards. He had a large trophy in his living room that the "Notre Dame Touchdown Club" had given him after they won the National Title there in 1977. He was genuinely proud. It was his only visible trophy of countless he has.

Coach told me that he was having problems remembering things, especially the players' names—and it was time to go. I reiterated that it was a sad day for all of us, but he seemed really at ease. He appeared so physically strong, and his house, yard, and swimming pool looked great. He was so happy that Toby had been so kind, and I again said we all knew what he had done by doing something that he had no professional experience and was not trained (broadcaster) and it became a labor of love for the University and the Sooner program.

Coach said he did not know when he could get

into his office. He said it is just like I left it and with the pandemic, and he did not know when he could "clear it out." He said a graduate assistant he thought was using it, and in typical Coach fashion, said he "hoped his things were not in the way." Always the gentleman.

He got a little reflective in our visit. He said, "Our family really liked it here and I liked him (Gary Gibbs). We did not want to move. Still like it here, Switzer just lives right over there (pointing)." He went into how hard he (Gary) worked, and he was good in game prep, but "really did not like the other stuff a Head Coach does, he still lives in Norman." Positive in all situations, as usual.

The University and Sooner Sports properties announced on the Friday before the first game (September 11, 2020) that Coach Merv was retiring from OU Football after 41 years. Forty-one years of being a coach, administrator, and broadcaster after 513 games.

Coach Merv and Michael Dean after his last
game Number 513. Little did we know.

I called Coach on the morning of the first game in 2020, (the next day) that he was not going to be in the booth, and he said he would not be attending. He was walking his regular three miles or so and sounded great. He was kind as always and inquired about me. He was genuinely sad that due to the pandemic, I was going to be doing the stats from home and using Google docs, and texts to give them the info for the game.

"They know how hard you will work for them," Coach quipped. He asked me if I still did my little write ups and sort for each game. I heartily said I would. He always makes you feel wanted and important, even if you have your doubts sometimes.

The accolades came in droves for Coach. He had been there for all those Bowls (33), conference championships (19) and even two National Championships 1985 and 2000. Coach had been around 382 wins at OU, (95 Switzer, 44 Gibbs, 5 Howie, 12 Blake, 190 Bob, and 36 with Lincoln.) That figures to over nine wins a year, which is incredible. Especially since there was one stretch in there when the Sooners only won 12 over three seasons. Coach had consistently said he had only been around four teams that had losing seasons (three at OU and one at Arkansas). He often proudly repeated that fact.

He was celebrated and I got to read my poem in my recorded feature during the broadcast vs Missouri State. I was able to say that I was lucky to be there for "over a hundred of those 513" and I got to tell him on air that I loved him. Toby said some wonderful things about how I had become close friends with Coach. Joe C said wonderful things on the TV broadcast and an era had ended in Sooner land.

Toby said that "We (Coach and I) could be seen on the road, sitting around cutting it up." No truer statement could have ever been worded. Toby put magic into words, exactly what I was thinking.

I got texts from friends during the broadcast. They wanted to know where Coach was. One of them said, after I said he had retired, "Can I sit with him at his house and let him tell me what he thinks?" That made me laugh. I could hear that familiar, "not really" in my head.

Coach watched the game at his daughter's house and really did not want to attend. His family bought Pay per View (think about that one) and it was the end of an era in Oklahoma football.

The 2020 season was strange. Due to Covid-19, there was a limit of people in the press box, thus I did all the home stats at my home via computer-text and email.

Covid did allow me plenty of time to develop some lists of Sooner statistics that are unique. I listed all the players (26) that had run, passed, and caught TD's while a Sooner dating back to 1943. It is an impressive list with Baker, Tommy McDonald, Little Joe Washington, Trevor Knight, Darrell Royal to name a few. I also completed my list of the players who scored a TD on their first ever carries with the Big Red. It has some little-known guys like Doug Switzer (Barry's son), Jaxson Uhles, and Mike Thomas who transferred to UNLV and became a NFL Washington Redskin star. It also listed a guy named Caleb Williams later on as well (2021).

We all drove to Lubbock for the Tech game on Halloween in 2020, with Toby, Drake, Greg, and me in Toby's "Landers" truck. Tech did not have the COVID-19 requirements, so I could do stats live. It was a great trip and was the last time we would ever get to travel with Greg Blackwood. He was so sick with pancreatic cancer and was only a shadow of himself. We all got to talk with him, but it was obvious that he would not be with us long. He was upbeat and had just gotten a new set of Ping irons and woods. He talked about playing with them. We had a fun time, but knew he was not going on any trips in the future. It still makes me cry to this day on the loss of this good man.

I have seen incredible things while doing all the Sooner games, but the positive and upbeat Greg Blackwood may have been the finest. He fought pancreatic cancer like no one I have ever seen. His ashes would now be placed with his mom's on Owen field, I hoped.

The 2020 Tech game and the aftermath was so indicative of the year. The Texas Tech visitors radio booth is next to a donor booth and has Tech fans (and apparently Sooners too) sitting in theatre like seats. There is no draping between them and us, and they can overlook us through a big glass during the game. We are so busy that we never look over and the angle of the booths are not conducive to paying attention to our neighbors.

After the game (a 62-28 win) we were doing a post-game show. A lady that had been (apparently) next door came running into our booth (reeking of alcohol) and virtually ran down and patted us all on the back and ran from the room. I am not sure how she got in, as the door is locked, or is shut. Most folks honor the broadcast and do not enter.

We all looked startled as our "space" was invaded since none of the guys had ever seen anything like it. Shortly thereafter, we all glanced next door as the woman who had run thru our booth was in there flashing her naked breasts and yelling Boomer Sooner. That will make you think and was very unexpected. No trip to Lubbock is ever ordinary, but it was Halloween.

Greg Trip Blackwood

I first met Gregor as a photographer and a journalistic winner,
we then began travelling, having fun, and enjoying many a dinner.
Driving thru the night in the Florida everglades,
to sitting in the glaring sun—in Ames in his shades.
Spotting all those jerseys and giving Toby the number,
he spent hours on field glasses as cool as a cucumber.
He always had a gadget or bracket or some recording device,
capturing what we are doing so others could see us nice.
There never is a time when someone did ask,
can you help me Greg, with even this menial task?
He always would say "sure brother",
then goes around looking to find out if there is another.
When the Sooners did roll out on Owen Field,
Greg Blackwood was there four hours early and never would yield.
The optimism and love for all he did came across,
made him so much like the man who gave it all on the cross.

I visited with Coach at his home in early December 2020, after the final game but before the Big XII Championship. Coach was in good spirits, and we watched the comeback win by Mizzou over Arkansas replayed on the television. Coach was commenting on the play and certain players. It was like old times.

We lamented about the death from cancer of Greg Blackwood. Greg had been a spotter since

2011 and was such a vital part of all we did. He was kind and always brought a sense of calm to the technical side of the broadcasts. Coach reflected that "He was such a nice person and a really good spotter, he really studied the names and numbers." No truer statement. "Can't win that cancer fight very often," Coach said. Simple fact.

We talked about the season and how the Sooners of 2020 had three games postponed. Army, WVU, and Tennessee. The games were postponed and were not later played and or rescheduled. That was the first time since the Spanish Flu epidemic of 1918. Sooners lost games to Texas, Mizzou, and Northwest Normal of Alva to postponement in 1918, there is an obvious overall uptick in scheduling in 2020, depending on how you look at WVU and or the Vols, and it is a slam to the Northwest Normal. The Sooners only played six games in 1918 and were undefeated. They only allowed seven points all year—to Phillips University's Haymakers from Enid, OK, winning 13-7. Phillips is now gone, and Northwest Normal is Northwestern Oklahoma State University. "I've never seen that," Coach said, about the postponements. "Hope it never happens again," he quipped. It had been the strangest of years.

I asked Coach if he had seen the commercial with Joe Montana and the final play against Houston in the Cotton Bowl. "No," he said, "I guess I became his guy (Joe Montana), he did not really get along with the head coach (Dan Devine)." He quipped that famous chuckle. Think about that one, Joe Montana's guy.

He was such a "Merv guy," he thanked him personally in 2000, in his acceptance speech when he joined the Pro Football Hall of Fame. What a tribute.

We then went to his clothes closet, and he showed me an array of his Sooner jackets and shirts. "Here take this one," he handed me a beautiful Oklahoma jacket and a sweatshirt from the 2016 Sugar Bowl. "I have so much of this stuff and other than my grandsons, I cannot use them all. They give me this stuff and there just is not enough days to wear them." I gladly walked out with the items, it was so Coach. Always giving.

He told me about how he was going to football practice a few times a week. He was walking over and sitting in the stands or walking on the sidelines. He said he liked the offensive line "but they may be too big. The weight was maybe taking their athletic agility away." I asked if he told the coaches, "No — oh no, just the guys standing around (him)."

When I left to go, he said he wished that I would have a good game down at the Big XII. He then said, "I can't lie in that I like watching the games at home for a change." We laughed about all the nights he sat in the postgame shows and laughed about all the times he said to me, "Wonder if anyone is listening," and I left to come home. It is sad to leave a legend, knowing his time is waning.

We had visited about Godly things and the study of the gospel and the meaning of it and the eternal life we want. I said it is so important to read it and do the best to adhere to its teachings. In his very authoritative Merv voice, he said, "That's exactly right."

I also told him of my recent studying the Bible with a man and baptizing him, and he was really pleased. His love for God and its teachings are always there.

It is hard to put into words what the seasons I spent with Coach Merv mean. His kind words, thoughtful compliments, and incredible Godly spirit have been one of the true blessings of my life. The firm hand on my shoulder or the warm handshake each week.

I continue finding myself sometimes daily thinking, "What would Coach say," or I wonder, "what he would think" and it makes me smile. The incredible thing is he never coached me a play in my life. He never saw me play, thank goodness, so he did not have to tell me, "You probably need to rethink this sport!"

Coach Merv Johnson treated me with respect, me, a slow footed, nearsighted guy from Weatherford, OK. Just like he does everyone else. It is why he is one of the most loved figures in all the annals of Oklahoma football.

Recently, I have had the pleasure of occasionally walking with him to practice from his home. He is so healthy and strong, and it is hard to keep up. He likes to walk by the dorms and frat houses and always comments, "Look at all the people from Texas we have" pointing to their car tags. We always laugh about us having something they want up here. What a gift to be with him.

He also reflected on seeing Brent Venables again as the new Sooner head coach. Coach said Brent had come over to him at the last practice and spent about thirty minutes catching up. "He did not need to do that," Coach said. "He is a heckuva guy and I am so happy for him." I am sure Coach was elated that Brent got the dream job. His job.

I have been so honored to sit alongside Coach for all those seasons, and I will never forget those famous words, spoken so humbly, honestly, "Not really."

Dennis G. "Stats" Kelly (Jr.) is a native of Sayre, Oklahoma. He is the rarest of Sooner fans who lived in Stillwater, OK and Austin, TX, luckily all before the age of seven. He spent other formable years in Mangum, OK and Weatherford, OK.

Kelly is a graduate of Weatherford High School, Southwestern Oklahoma State University with a B.S in Accounting, and also holds a Master of Arts from the University of Oklahoma. He is a Certified

Public Accountant with a long career as a Controller, Auditor, and Financial Manager.

Dennis has three daughters. Allison Kelly Harms, Kelsey Kelly Carter, and Denise Elaine Kelly. Five grandchildren, Vivian Ruth Carter, Lylah Denise Harms, Andrew Harms, Griffin Carter, and Harper Harms. Kelly now lives in Edmond, OK with his wife Elaine Denson Kelly, and daughter Denise. He has, since 2011, provided stats for the Sooner Football Radio broadcasts.